IMAGES
of America

ENGLEWOOD
AND ENGLEWOOD CLIFFS

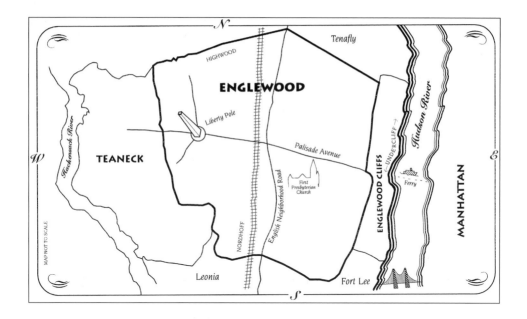

ACKNOWLEDGMENTS

This book was researched, planned, and written by the Friends of the Englewood Library Centennial Book Committee: Bobbie Bouton-Goldberg, Arnold Brown, Mary Buchbinder, Betty Grossman, Lisa Levien, and Irmari Nacht.

When Betty Grossman presented the idea for this book we all agreed it would be a good project. We never dreamed it would involve so many hours of work. We would like to give special thanks to the following whose generous and professional help shortened those hours and shaped this book: Farah Farhadian, Robert Griffin, Len Hansen, Eleanor Harvey, Dr. William Lee, Dr. John K. Lattimer, John McLoughlin, Eric Nelsen, John Spring, and Elizabeth Torjussen.

In addition, we would like to thank those who helped with photographs, maps, and information: Ahavath Torah, Ken Albert, The American Red Cross, Natalie Beaumont, Bergen County Historical Society, Fred Binder, Sandra Borg, Bill Boyan, Frances Brown, Dick Burnon, Ben Cohen, Ann Davis, Charles Dillon, Dwight Englewood School, Whittie English Jr., Elisabeth Morrow School, Englewood Board of Education, Englewood Field Club, Englewood School of Nursing (archives), Peg Escher, First Presbyterian Church, Edna Floyd, Galilee United Methodist Church, Phil Goldberg, Dustin Griffin, Lee Hecht, Ruth Herrick, the Ted Holmes Collection, Don Horsey, Joan Van Alstyne Johnson, Edith Kaske, Lorraine Kephart, Marty Lebson, J.K. Levien, Perry Levinsohn, Ellen Luthin, David Mammone, Olga Mosciaro, Mostly Digital, Jeremy Nacht, Carl Nutzhorn, Father Joseph O'Brien, Florence Passantino, Martine Rawson, the Palisades Interstate Park Commission, *The Record*, Robert F. Ryder, St. Paul's Episcopal Church, Marilyn Salame, Rhoda Sidney, Sisters of St. Joseph, Rev. Howard Sterling, John Stillman, Millie Sturm, Warrenita Tibbs, the Tinsley Family, Janet Van Alstyne, Marianne Wattley, the Weidig Family, Jeanette Wides, Dave Wright, Gloria Wyman, and Dr. Barbara Wiklinski.

We couldn't have put this together without the support and help of Don Jacobsen, Charlene Scaringello, and the great staff of the Englewood Library.

IMAGES
of America

ENGLEWOOD
AND ENGLEWOOD·CLIFFS

Bobbie Bouton-Goldberg, Arnold Brown,
Mary Buchbinder, Betty Grossman,
Lisa Levien, and Irmari Nacht

ARCADIA

First published 1998
Reprinted 2004

Published by Arcadia Publishing,
Charleston SC, Chicago IL, Portsmouth NH, San Francisco CA

Printed in Great Britain

Library of Congress Catalog Card Number: 98-88407

For all general information, contact Arcadia Publishing:
Telephone 843-853-2070
Fax 843-853-0044
E-mail sales@arcadiapublishing.com
For customer service and orders:
Toll-free 1-888-313-2665

Visit us on the Internet at www.arcadiapublishing.com

CONTENTS

6

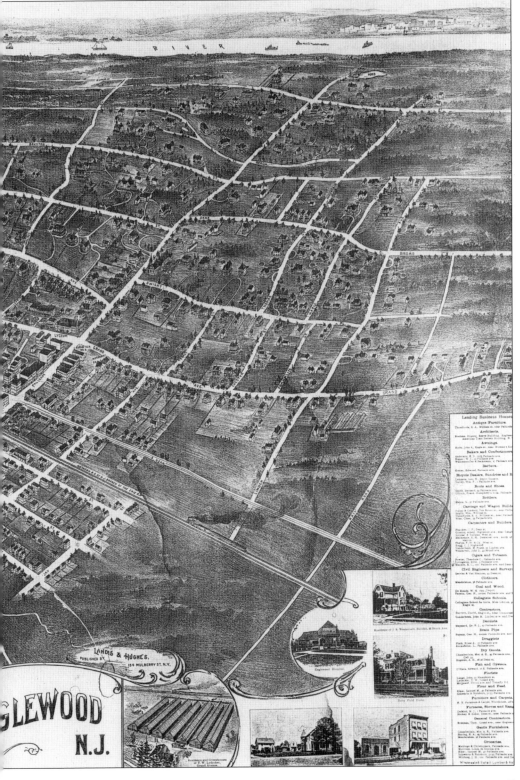

INTRODUCTION

Englewood and Englewood Cliffs, perched atop the Palisades overlooking the Hudson River across from New York City, are communities with a shared history. Indeed, until the 1890s, Englewood Cliffs and Teaneck were part of Englewood township, as were smaller hamlets called Nordhoff (aka Walton) and Highwood. Englewood was roughly divided east and west by the railroad tracks, and into wards by a cross of the RR and Palisade Avenue. Within these areas there were neighborhoods, the first ward's The Hill and East Hill; the second ward's South Hills and Floraville; and a cluster of neighborhoods at the juncture of the third and fourth ward, Lappland, Texas, and Liberty Pole.

We chose photographs that would tell the story of Englewood's diverse past. We found photographs in family collections, libraries, newspaper files, and through historic societies. We went to house and estate sales, foraged through attics and garages, met people on hiking trails who knew someone who knew someone, spent hours in archives of libraries looking at old books, and spoke with hundreds of people.

The chapters are arranged chronologically into three time periods: *Early Englewood*, with its Dutch houses and farms, and settlements on the Hudson; *the Coming of the Railroad* (1859–1899), a transition from farm to village to small elegant city; and *the Bedroom of Wall Street* (1900–1931), the horse, the trolley, the ferry, the car, and the end of an era with the George Washington Bridge. Within the chapters, we grouped related pictures; each two-page spread tells a unified story. Our themes are transportation and change, the devastating effect of fires, and the Ciceronian ideals of the founders of Englewood and Englewood Cliffs: do well in business, build a church, and plant a tree.

As several local historians read this book and new information was unearthed, captions changed. The final decision on historical veracity was ours. Some captions relate incidental but fascinating information beyond the scope of the accompanying photographs. We found that we were seeing the area with new awareness, noting architectural details and appreciating the past. We hope that readers will be likewise motivated.

Although the book ends in the 1930s, it foreshadows the diversity and uniqueness that is Englewood today, on this the centennial celebration of the incorporation of "the Queen City of the Palisades," once the "Bedroom of Wall Street," and now "A Progressive Community."

One

EARLY ENGLEWOOD

The virtually impassable Palisades were deeply wooded, home to abundant wildlife. Farms in the valley were widely spaced, surrounded by pastures and swamps. The entire population shared a small number of names. Running from the Hudson to the Hackensack Rivers, the area that became Englewood encompassed part of English Neighborhood and Liberty Pole. Hackensack Township recorded births, marriages, deaths, and land conveyances. The local Squire served as justice of the peace, magistrate, trustee, and general superintendent of village affairs.

LIBERTY POLE TAVERN. In 1766, to celebrate the repeal of the Stamp Act, local colonists erected a flagpole topped by a liberty cap, symbol of freedom, at the junction of the King's Highway (now Palisade Avenue), Lafayette Avenue, and Tenafly Road. By 1776, as George Washington's military map indicates, the neighborhood was known as Liberty Pole. After the Revolution, the Liberty Pole Tavern and its successors served as post office and stop for Linus Rider's stage line to the Hoboken Ferry. Ladies had quilting bees upstairs, downstairs men drank applejack. At elections, males voted out loud. Dinner and horse racing on Tenafly Road followed.

LIBERTY UNION SCHOOL C. 1818. The school was built adjacent to Liberty Pole Tavern by Peter Westervelt for the Liberty Union School Company on land donated by John Benson and James Lydecker "wholly and solely for the purpose of a seminary for the education and instruction of youth." The school welcomed different religious denominations. Moses Hall was paid $85 per school quarter to teach the familiar names Westervelt, Brinckerhoff, Vanderbeek, Lydecker, Cole, Durie, DeMott, and Van Buskirk. The school was later moved stone by stone to 486 Tenafly Road, and is now a residence.

Old Revolutionary House. Englewood, N. J.

REVOLUTIONARY WAR HOUSE. In 1776, George Washington informed the Continental Congress he'd be staying across from the Liberty Pole Tavern for two or three days while his army foraged. It was at Liberty Pole after the Revolution that Alexander Hamilton, Washington's aide-de-camp, proposed rewriting the Articles of Confederation in the first known written request for a new constitution. The house was later known as the Tunis Cooper homestead and then became the home of Dr. Valentine Ruch Jr., chief physician to WW I Camp Merritt. Now it is the site of a small shopping center.

GARRETT LYDECKER HOUSE C. 1803, ENGLISH NEIGHBORHOOD ROAD. In 1705, a patent was granted to Gerrit Lydecker for the land that formed the nucleus of the future Englewood. One of his descendants, Thomas, who as a boy of 15 fled from advancing British armies across the Hackensack River with a wagon full of family treasures, returned and rebuilt the family homestead on this site. In 1922 there were six living Englewood descendants of Ryck Lydecker, the founding father of the family, who emigrated from Holland in 1660. Now, it is the Southeast Senior Center for Independent Living.

HENRICK BRINCKERHOFF HOUSE C. 1735, TEANECK ROAD. Henrick Brinckerhoff built this squat 11-room Dutch Colonial with four fireplaces, as well as slave quarters in one upstairs section. (Slaves and free blacks were almost 20 percent of the population of Bergen County by 1776.) The location was close to Overpeck Creek, where melons grown on this 1600s farm were loaded onto boats for New York. In 1891, this area split off from Englewood and became Teaneck. Brinckerhoff-Demarest descendants lived here until 1990.

THOMAS DEMAREST HOUSE, ENGLISH NEIGHBORHOOD ROAD. Thomas Demarest was born in Englewood in 1817, the son of Reverend Dominie Demarest and Margaret Lydecker, and married another one of the prolific Lydecker descendants. He farmed and also served as Hackensack Freeholder (1849), state senator (1854), Speaker of the House (1855), and for ten years was Bergen County Clerk. He secured the right of way and the contract to build the Northern Railroad; he served as president and treasurer.

THOMPSON RESIDENCE C. 1800S. This structure was next to a church on English Neighborhood Road (now Grand Avenue). During the Revolution the English Neighborhood Road was known as King's Highway and turned west following the present Palisade Avenue to Liberty Pole, then down Lafayette. Note the wooden sidewalk and the cow in the side yard. Most households kept livestock and had market gardens. Until 1859 the only grocery was Van Brunt's store, 1 mile south of the village. After the advent of the railroad household heads would carry their baskets on the train and buy provisions in New York City.

DeMott-Westervelt House c. 1808, English Neighborhood Road. The main stone section was built by Henry DeMott for his daughter, the wife of Peter Westervelt, a descendant of Lubbert Lubbeertsen Van Westervelt, who landed in New Amsterdam from Holland in 1662. Peter added the frame wing just before his marriage. The house, occupied by Westervelts for 185 years, then became, along with the barn in the orchard, a private nursery school and later the Leonard Johnson Day Care Center. It is now part of the Patriot Centre.

John G. Benson Home c. 1800. This house is situated on land confiscated after the War of Independence from a Tory, Reverend Garret Lydecker, and sold to Benson, a captain in the U.S. Militia. Benson married Maria, the widow of Garret Lydecker's cousin Cornelius, and built this house. They enjoyed "a meadow which produced the best English hay, a fine orchard of choice apples, and five acres of salt meadow nigh the homestead." It is now the headquarters of the American Red Cross.

DeMott House, 488 Grand Avenue. The Huguenot Matthais DeMott settled lower English Neighborhood in 1685. His grandson Jacob was a Hackensack Freeholder in 1769. The smaller section of this sandstone building, one room down, one room up, is the oldest structure in Englewood (*c.* 1730). The rest of the house was built in 1760. The family lived downstairs and slept upstairs in an open loft. Usually Dutch colonials face south, but this house faces east on (then) English Neighborhood Road. The windows have fewer panes of glass at their tops.

H.E. and J. Taylor's Stables on Dean Street. By 1887 this building also housed Dr. John Turnure's veterinary practice. The same year this stable was the starting point of an English hunt led by Dr. Hardy Banks. "Hounds, high-bred horses and a fox loosed to the course" galloped to Schraalenburgh South Church. Local farmers objected. The hunt disbanded two years later. In 1889, Jacob Taylor rented his horses to the fire department at $2 per horse per fire and trained untied horses to run to their suspended harnesses at the clang of the fire bell.

14

CAPT. VON WAGONER'S HOME. This house was located in Fishers Village, a part of the Undercliff settlement of approximately 800 people (1850) that stretched for 10 miles along the Hudson River at the foot of the Palisades. After the Revolutionary War, this area, originally settled by Dutch families, became a busy shipping port. Nearby lumbermen pitched trees down the cliffs to be used in local boat building or floated the logs to New York City for firewood.

FISHERS VILLAGE. Capt. Charles Von Wagoner is shown drying fishing nets. Fishing was the main occupation in Undercliff. Spring shad fishing was often profitable enough to support a family all year. The Captain's wife, Susan, is buried in the Undercliff cemetery. Nearby is Pickletown, named in the 1830s when a sloop laden with cucumbers capsized. Thrifty local housewives pickled the cucumbers that washed ashore. Other local families included Allison, Bloomer, Westervelt, Coverley, Huyler, Beckert, VanScrivener, Norman, Willey, Crum, Jackson, and Brown.

JOHN VAN BRUNT (1802–1879). Superintendent of education for 20 years and a two-term state senator, he also organized the Bergen County Mutual Assurance Association, and, with Thomas Demarest, parented the Northern Railroad, of which he was secretary, treasurer, and director. He owned the general store at Forest and Grand. In 1860, his Palisade Avenue building, pictured above, held Squire Miller's offices, the first post office (he was postmaster), and his second store, where a meeting was held to choose a name for the new town. "Paliscena" and "Brayton" were suggested, and "Englewood" was chosen.

VAN BRUNT HOMESTEAD C. 1834. Peter Westervelt Jr. built this home for his daughter Margaret, who married John Van Brunt and had eight children. In its day, this farm was the showplace of the township. People would stay here and at the Dominie Demarest farm; there were no hotels. J. Wyman Jones and his family spent the summer of 1859 here while Jones platted the future town.

16

Two

THE COMING
OF THE RAILROAD

The railroad "roared up the valley like an uncaged lion." The advent of the railroad changed the sleepy bucolic northern valley forever. In 1859, a visitor saw "Well cultivated farms, [which] sloped down the valley from the west . . . orchards of golden fruit . . . scattered dwellings of peaceful farmers . . . densely wooded Palisades . . . nature in all her glorious dress . . . love at first sight." Soon farmlands were bought and sold. Land bought for $150 an acre sold the next week for $900. In the village area where there were no trees, no drainage and plenty of mosquitoes, trees were planted, roads macadamized, huge houses erected, schools and churches established, hotels opened to become meeting places, organizations founded, and services increased. In 1899, Englewood was incorporated as a city.

1887 STATION. The Northern Railroad connected to the Erie for national access at Piermont, New York. The first train through Englewood ran south to Jersey City in May 1859. One train ran each way daily. By fall, three ran daily except Sunday. Englewood had three stations named for their locations: Nordhoff, Englewood, and Highwood. Trains would "stop on signal" at Van Brunt's shed 1 mile south of Englewood station.

ENGLEWOOD GREETINGS. Wood-burning locomotives sent sparks, burning a strip 50 feet on either side of the track. Englewood, as midpoint of the line, had wood, steam sawmills, and ties piled along the tracks. Logs were hauled down Palisade Avenue, then a lumbering road. The conductor would refresh himself at Stagg's while the train took on firewood and water. Carpenter shops sprang up near the stations in anticipation of new building. By 1870, when the Palisades were deforested, coal replaced wood.

FREIGHT STATION C. 1910. Originally built as a second main passenger station, it was located opposite city hall. Highwood Station, between Hudson Avenue and Ivy Lane, had a large freight house just to its south. In 1897, railroad gates were positioned at the Palisade Avenue crossing. Prior to this, Timothy Hickey would yell, "look out," in stentorian tones to warn of approaching trains. People were hired to "shoo" geese and goats off the track.

ENGLEWOOD STATION 1898. Above is the third Englewood station, which boasted a 13-by-16-foot ladies retiring room. Forty-six trains ran daily round-trips serving over 6,000 commuters. Stations were built on either side of the track with a connecting tunnel for the safety of those needing to cross the track. In 1920, a trainmen's strike occurred. *The New York Times* reported that Englewood commuters served as conductors and engineers kept the trains running.

ENGLEWOOD HOUSE 1860. This was Englewood's "real estate exchange." Nathan T. Johnson, J. Wyman Jones, and I. Smith Homans bought 3 acres on Engle Street and hired Andrew Demarest to build a hotel to attract and shelter newcomers while their houses were being built. For 37 years it was both "home" and social center, with bowling, billiards, receptions, and "hops." It was used by private schools until 1902, then was bought by the city for public school purposes. Later torn down for Franklin school, it is now the site of the Englewood Library.

J.WYMAN JONES (1822–1904).
Jones, a young lawyer in his
thirties, having heard about a
proposed railroad, visited the
northern valley area in 1857 and
selected Englewood as a choice
spot. He purchased 125 acres
from Overpeck Creek to the
Hudson River and spearheaded
the purchase of 625 additional
acres. He was instrumental in
naming the town, building the
first railroad station, and
encouraging his wealthy New
York City and Brooklyn friends to
join him. He was called "the father
of Englewood."

JONES ESTATE. Built *c.* 1860 on 20 acres, Jones's house, "Erdenheim," and carriage house, both
pink sandstone in a Greek Revival style with distinctive stepped gables, are still standing, but
there are many more houses on subdivisions between them. Jones, a fancier of all things Celtic,
planted large quantities of Abbottsford ivy.

J.A. HUMPHREY HOUSE. This house, built in the spring of 1860 on 6 acres, was the first home in the new village of Englewood. During construction the family boarded at J.W. Deuell's boys school. Daughter Mai, born in 1859, was the first birth in the village. In a charming book, published in 1899, Humphrey states, "The object of the founders of Englewood was to build a town of substantial homes, where peace and happiness might dwell."

PALISADE HOUSE. Built in 1868, this hotel was on the southeast corner of Palisade Avenue and Dean Street. Owned by veterinarian John Turnure, it flourished until the "arid days" of Prohibition. It was sometimes used as a community center, for township or public meetings, as a polling place, and as the site of more than one hot primary contest. It closed in 1947.

YOUNG LADIES SEMINARY C. 1860. Located on the Dominie Demarest Farm, the seminary was run by William Dwight, brother of Reverend Dwight, and music professor Jonathan Fowler. Miss Gerard, a drawing mistress at the school, painted the picture of the Chapel on page 24. The school became quite popular, attracting both local and boarding students. Many of these young ladies were received into Englewood society; a few married and remained. The structure burned in 1867, and later the Lyceum was built on this site.

KURSTEINER SCHOOL. Early in the 1860s, Dr. August Kursteiner, a Swiss American, taught at Rev. George Grey's school in the old Benson house. Rev. Grey accepted day students and boarders. In 1867, Kursteiner founded his own school and boarding house on 4 acres between Liberty Road and Palisade Avenue. Although his doctoral degree was in music, he had a broad education and his school, grades one through 13, prepared young men for college.

Jacob A. Bogert House 1867. This Carpenter Gothic house still stands on the corner of Tenafly Road and Henry Street. Bogert, a bricklayer and plasterer, built it, ten houses on Henry Street, and also worked on the Lyceum. In the 1870s, Bogert was the town tax collector. At a 50th anniversary celebration of Englewood in 1920, Bogert, a resident for more than 70 years, received a gold badge.

Andrew D. Bogert House, 1862, Tenafly Road at Demarest Avenue. Bogert (1835–1918) trained at Cooper Union and had a carpenter shop on Palisade Avenue. A contracting builder like Henry Jones and Moses Springer, Bogert built the Athenaeum, Palisade Mountain House, and the hospital. In 1873, he was chairman of the township committee, in 1895 he became a county freeholder, and in 1902 he became city treasurer.

FIRST PRESBYTERIAN CHURCH, 1860. A group of religious-minded early settlers, who had been meeting in local houses and schools, raised money to build this chapel on Palisade Avenue on the first rise of the East Hill. By a 14 to 3 vote, they chose a Presbyterian form of church government. Their first pastor, Rev. James Harrison Dwight, a Yale graduate who attended both medical school and the seminary, received $750 per annum. When the congregation outgrew its walls, the chapel was dismantled and reconstructed at Brookside Cemetery.

FIRST PRESBYTERIAN CHURCH C. 1890. In 1870, an elaborate Victorian Gothic Revival sandstone structure seating 800 worshippers replaced the original chapel. Later there were extensive alterations and additions, including the Vermilye Chapel. The history of the church is intertwined with the history of Englewood, as many of the prominent and affluent families including Jones, Van Brunt, Phelps, Humphrey, Homans, Brinckerhoff, and Morrow were members. During its first 25 years the church collected $387,000 for charitable causes.

Dear Pearl This is the church we attend Lovingly Grace

METHODIST CHURCH, 1869. Scattered followers of Wesley moved here from Jersey City holding cottage prayer meetings under the leadership of John Westervelt of Tenafly until Dr. Daniel Wise, an affluent, enterprising Methodist preacher, helped them raise building funds. Andrew Bogert and Thomas Dole built the city's second church at 20 Grand Avenue for $2,250 on land donated by J. Wyman Jones.

HIGHLAND UNION SUNDAY SCHOOL. In April of 1874, in a meeting at William Vermilye's home, parents of the West Side neighborhood founded the Highland Sunday School. Like many other early congregations, they held classes in the public school. In 1875, Jacob Vermilye gave them $1,500 to purchase a lot on Hudson Avenue and they lost no time in putting up a small church mortgaged for $3,000. In 1900 the name changed to Highwood Reformed Church. It later became the Community Church.

CHRISTIAN REFORMED CHURCH, 1875. During the late 1860s, worshippers of the True Dutch Reformed Church held meetings in Englewood Hall, the third-floor assembly room in the W. Palisade Avenue building owned by Joseph Stagg. When they had saved enough money, they hired John Voorhis, a carpenter living on Demarest Avenue, to build their graceful church at Tenafly Road and Demarest Avenue. Later they ordained him as minister.

ST. CECILIA'S ROMAN CATHOLIC CHURCH, DEDICATED 1866. Parishioners met in a Waldo Place house and then shared time with a Protestant congregation in a city-owned building that later became the police lockup. Their priest walked 2 1/2 miles from Fort Lee. Fifty people raised $850 for land at Waldo and Division Street and hired Andrew Bogert as the builder. "Obliged to send our help to Fort Lee in our own carriages in order to retain them in our employ," affluent homeowners contributed to the building fund.

CARRIAGE FACTORY, ESTABLISHED 1883. Charles West operated a carriage factory, a blacksmith shop, and later a garage on the street named for him. Englewood had another carriage factory, with a steam saw mill built by Joseph Stagg, north of the city center along the railroad. There was also one silk mill that lasted a short time and a small furniture industry. There were no large industries in Englewood.

NATIONAL HOTEL C. 1890. The hotel was located two blocks west of the trolley at 30 Palisade Avenue. Various hotel ads mention an attached livery stable and meals at all hours with first-class wines, liquors, and "seegars." It was one of 12 hotels listed in the 1903 Business Directory. Others include Roadside Hotel in Nordhoff, Bijou Hotel on Palisade, Lafayette Hotel on Lafayette, Waldo Hotel on Waldo, and the Railroad Hotel on Van Brunt.

WILLIAM WALTER PHELPS (1839–1894). Valedictorian of his Columbia Law School class and owner of more railroads than Harriet Beecher Stowe said she could count, Phelps was elected to Congress in 1872 and helped enact legislation to suppress the KKK. He was Minister to Austria and to Germany, served again in Congress and was appointed to New Jersey's highest court. By 1891, he owned 4,000 acres from the Hudson to the Hackensack and at his death he owned half the land in Teaneck.

THE GRANGE C. 1886. William Walter Phelps's 350-foot-long mansion was the centerpiece of his 1,500-acre "Englewood Farm." Phelps expanded the old farmhouse on the former Garrett Brinckerhoff farm to include a library, billiard room, music room, picture gallery, and a fireplace so tall a man could stand in it. The notable guest list included President Ulysses S. Grant. The Grange burned in 1888 and the ruins were a tourist attraction for years. Teaneck's municipal complex now occupies the site.

RUSTIC BRIDGE, MACKAY PARK C. 1908. Phelps made many improvements to his land before part of it became Mackay Park. He built 60 little bridges of wood and stone and planted over 600,000 trees. Phelps allowed public use of his roads 364 days a year if it didn't interfere with "the superior rights of birds and small game to this, their home." In the summer months his 30 miles of paved road lined with trees and flowers were a mecca for thousands.

MACKAY PARK ENTRANCE C. 1908. Mayor Donald Mackay's 1906 Christmas gift to the City of Englewood was a large tract of land in the Fourth Ward to be used as a park. Mackay purchased this land from W.W. Phelps. This entrance includes the only remaining (of six) Phelps gatehouse. Later, more land was added to the park. In his will Mackay bequeathed $10,000 for maintenance.

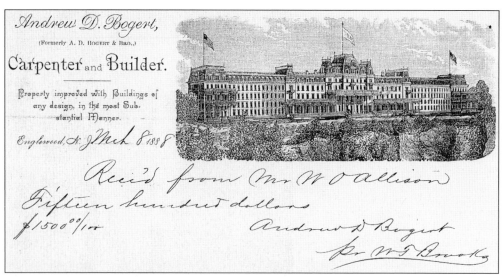

PALISADES MOUNTAIN HOUSE C. 1870. One of the world's finest summer hotels was situated beautifully at the top of the Palisades opposite Spuyten Duyvil. Built by William Dana and Senator Cornelius Lydecker, it was 600 feet long and could accommodate 500 guests. Amenities included full orchestras playing morning and evening, a billiard hall, bowling alley, celebrated cuisine, and salubrious country air. The hotel burned in 1884. The Sisters of St. Joseph now own the property.

DANA MANSION, "GREYCLIFF," C. 1861. Much of the building material was prefabricated in Boston, delivered by schooner, and hauled up the cliff. William Dana, a publisher, was brother-in-law to J. Wyman Jones. Mrs. Dana, the "Lady on the Hill," was known for her charitable work. They became foster parents to William O. Allison, who added his middle name, Outis, to gratify Mrs. Dana, matching his initials to those of her pen name Olive A. Wadsworth. "Greycliff" was destroyed to make way for the Palisades Interstate Parkway.

WILLIAM O. ALLISON. Born in 1849 in Undercliff, Allison rose from the foot of the cliff to the top. He worked as a reporter, started his own weekly, became a banker, and invested in land along the Palisades. Defeated in his bid for road commissioner, Allison sued Englewood disputing the voting rights of female landowners and the service of a female election clerk. Allison won, but dissatisfied with Englewood, he instigated the 1895 secession of Englewood Cliffs and was elected its first mayor. Thirty-three voters elected 14 officials.

ALLISON MANSION C. 1885. Allison built a mansion designed by J. Cleveland Cady, architect of the Metropolitan Opera house, on the site of the Palisades Mountain House. It burned in 1903. After Allison's death in 1924, much of the land he owned near his beloved Palisades was donated to the public, including Allison Park overlooking the Hudson, and Allison Park along Jones Road.

COE MANSION. Located on the lip of the Palisades north of the Dana Mansion was the second house of George S. Coe, distant kin to John Alden and president of American Exchange Bank. His brother William, a Civil War captain, organized Englewood's Protection Society and Militia Company. In 1886, William's sons George and Louis tackled a robber at the Teaneck schoolhouse. George was shot and a manhunt ensued. Citizens demanded formal police protection.

TAYLOR-BLISS HOUSE C. 1878. Located in the Highwood section on the NE corner of Engle Street is this flamboyant example of the Second Empire style. In 1912, Archibald Taylor, its first owner, sold it to Delos Bliss, general manager of a Jersey City lumber company and vice president of Palisade Trust and Guaranty Company. Bliss's daughter Laura married Thomas B. Cuming, a noted athlete. The house was completely restored in 1984.

RESIDENCE OF MRS. DONALD MACKAY, DWIGHT PLACE C. 1890. There were about 50 great houses located in Englewood, most on grounds of 20 to 30 acres. Many mansions remain but the land has been sub-divided. Mrs. Jennie Wise Mackay held title to this Stick Style mansion and its surrounding property in her own name and as such, even before suffrage, was entitled to vote in property-based referendums. This house no longer exists.

DONALD MACKAY. Mackay worked on Wall Street as Colonel Vermilye's partner and became president of the Stock Exchange. He was president of the Protection Society, president of Citizen's National Bank, a founder of the fire department, and mayor from 1906 to 1910. His gifts to Englewood include Mackay Park and the first library building. In 1910, at his 70th birthday dinner, a grateful city presented him with a silver loving cup.

GEORGE W. BETTS RESIDENCE, 162 CEDAR ST. C. 1870. This is a Second Empire house with unusual incised ornamentation and cutout trim. Betts, active in St. Paul's Church, headed a paint company, the Sewer Company, and the Improvement Association. Citizens would fund projects and later create formal associations. To drain Palisade Avenue from the Lyceum to the creek below Englewood Avenue, a sewer was privately built and maintained. The Improvement Society planted trees, lighted streets, removed rubbish, helped the poor, formed a bank, then became the Improvement Association.

HOWLAND-BARBER HOUSE, 42 LINCOLN STREET C. 1868. This stone mansion with stables, staff cottage, and two gatehouses is the second house built by Francis Howland, a lawyer who left the Cotton Exchange to develop Englewood real estate. Howland, Homans, and Phelps purchased large tracts of land as the Three-Third Account. Phelps paid cash; the others assumed liabilities. In 1885, Herbert Barber, owner of the "most important concern in the shipping industry," bought the house.

34

CIVIL WAR VETS. Pictured are Henry G. Demarest (not in uniform), Charles Barr, Mr. Christie, and one unidentified veteran. During the Civil War, Nathan T. Johnson (later state senator) organized "Home Guards." They drilled upstairs in Andrew Bogert's carpenter shop. Rumors of a Confederate attack on Englewood turned out to be farm wagons heading to Liberty Pole Tavern for a political gathering. Englewood and Walton (later Nordhoff) became Company I, of the 989-man 22nd Regiment of the Infantry (Bergen County).

J. FRANK HOWELL HOUSE C. 1867. J. Frank Howell, his wife, Mary Cornelia, and his daughter Mary lived in the Third Ward's most elaborate example of Second Empire architecture, located on Liberty Road opposite Reis Avenue. Howell, a stockbroker who boarded cavalry horses during the Spanish-American War, was active in WW I fund drives. Englewood's quota was $5.5 million; however, it raised $8.5 million. Howell was instrumental in creating Veterans Memorial Park with its WW I memorial plinth.

ATHENAEUM 1869. On the northwest corner of Palisade Avenue and Engle Street, this three-story brick building built as Englewood's opera house included an 800-seat auditorium, stores, and Smith's School. After its gala standing room only opening with opera star Clara Kellogg, it was never more than a pretentious white elephant. It burned to the ground in 1887. Smith's school never reopened. The resourceful Mrs. Chamberlain, a first floor store owner, eventually built a dry goods emporium on Palisade Avenue.

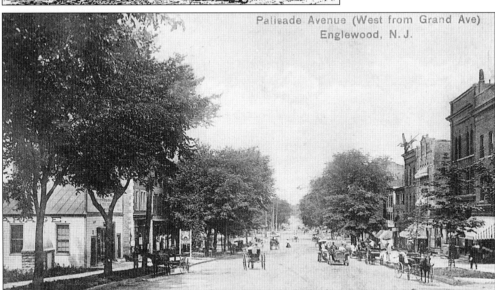

Palisade Avenue (West from Grand Ave) Englewood, N.J.

EARLY PALISADE AVENUE. At this time, Humphrey owned most of the Fourth Ward south of Palisade Avenue. In 1860, 6 to 8 marsh acres were acquired and 12 small double "bathhouses" were built for working men. The landlord collected rent by raft in rainy weather. Later these houses were relocated along the railroad tracks. There were "Irish Evictions"; if a tenant didn't pay his rent, the landlord disassembled the house. By 1876, Palisade Avenue, although still unpaved, had commercial buildings, stores, churches, and three hotels.

LYCEUM C. 1890. Located on the northeast corner of Engle Street and Palisade Avenue, the former site of the Demarest farmhouse, it was designed by J. Cleveland Cady, architect of the New York Museum of Natural History, to take over some functions of the Athenaeum. It contained a bank in the tower, a ballroom, an auditorium, a gentlemen's club on the second floor, and three library rooms, one for men, one for women, and one for singing.

ENGLE STREET SHOWING BANK, ENGLEWOOD, N. J.

ENGLE STREET. Tillotson's Directory lists physicians, storeowners, and civil engineers residing on 60-by-150-foot lots on both sides of unpaved Engle Street north of Palisade Avenue. By 1900, it was strongly felt that a workingman should own his own residence. Nearby on James Street, builders, clerks, plumbers, and carpenters lived in two-story wooden frame houses.

LAYING WATER PIPES, 1886. By 1885, people were tired of wells running dry and paying $1 per load of water. The Hackensack Water Company made a deviation from the New Milford to the Hoboken line, and by 1887 Englewood had an abundance of pure water from the Hackensack River's headwaters. Water pressure problems east of Lydecker (a house burned when water couldn't reach the second floor) necessitated adding a high-pressure pumping station.

ROCKEFELLER PHARMACY. The pharmacy was established in 1871 by Lucius Rockefeller in one of the stores of Palisade House. This "true drug shop" also sold "family cough syrup of tar, liquorice and wild cherry," gifts, and "soda that satisfies, never satiates." By 1899, Rockefeller was supplying Englewood Hospital and private customers with oxygen.

1890 PARADE. Englewood has had many parades to celebrate holidays such as July 4th and Decoration Day, and special events, such as a parade for Olympic skating champion Dick Button. The granddaddy of all parades was probably the parade celebrating Ulysses S. Grant's election. Grand Marshall Henry Banks led bands and citizens who paraded on foot, on horseback, and in carriages throughout the city, past patriotically decorated houses, then down Palisade Avenue to the ballpark near Humphrey Street.

PALISADE AVENUE. This street was planned in 1859 as a "100-foot street." In 1862, a stream-fed ravine opposite the Presbyterian church was filled. Paved with cobblestones in sections from 1911 to 1916, Palisade Avenue became an interstate artery when the Dyckman Street ferry connected with Englewood Cliffs in 1915. The wide flagstone sidewalks were narrowed to enlarge the roadway. Electric poles were erected in 1899 amid considerable controversy. In a 1901 protest, Dan Platt cut down the poles near his home.

HOSPITAL. On March 8, 1888, Mrs. Sheppard Homans and William Blaikie held a meeting to discuss building a small hospital and formed a committee of six men and six women. On May 7, 1888, they obtained a site south of Brookside Cemetery, opposite the Field Club and running from Engle Street to the railroad. In 1890, Andrew Bogert built a small wooden building with 12 beds for $5,000. That first year 75 patients were treated. Revenues were $4,672.09, expenditures $4,208.37, leaving a profit of $463.72.

NURSING SCHOOL, 1896. It was difficult and expensive to hire nurses from New York, so the hospital established a two-year on-site program to train nurses in public health, administration, and social service. After training one month, a nurse would give anesthesia, take charge of the operating room, and do many tasks now considered advanced skills. The first class had three students. The second class, pictured, had twice that number.

CAROLINE HELEN VAN HORNE, M.D. (1862–1914).
In 1897, "Dr. Carrie" began a private general
practice in Englewood in partnership with her
brother Byron, "Dr. Van Horne." She was
awarded hospital privileges and served on the
Englewood Hospital Board. In 1899, the
Bergen County Medical Society elected her
its first woman member. Notes from the
Society state, "Her cheerful face
combined with her confident manner in
the sickroom contributed largely to her
professional success."

DAISY FIELDS HOME FOR CRIPPLED CHILDREN. In 1893, Mr. and Mrs. Herbert Turner bought
the Banta Homestead standing in 4 acres of daisies on Central Avenue and remodeled it to
provide long-term care for children recovering from tubercular bone disease. Englewood's
wealthy donated steadily; they came with dollars, fresh fruit, vegetables, milk, toys, clothing,
bedding, entertainment, and always, cartons of candy. By 1928, when area hospitals assumed
more responsibility the home closed.

ENGLEWOOD WOMEN'S CLUB. Presently located at the former Brinckerhoff Carriage House, the club was formed in 1895 by 18 women and divided into departments of civics, literature, current events, economics, and political study. Their objective was good fellowship and cooperation with municipal government. In 1915, tired of walking across town and up the hill, the West Side townswomen began an offshoot organization. They sold so many war bonds that a warplane was named the Contemporary Club of Englewood.

THE ENGLEWOOD CLUB. Incorporated in 1891 with 61 charter members, the club purchased the 115 Palisade Avenue home of an Englewood founder, I. Smith Homans, for $25,000. Their motto was "character, fellowship, service." This men-only club cost $50 to join and dues were $25. Use of the billiard table cost 30¢ per hour, and pool cues were 3¢ per game. A full-time staff pampered permanent bachelor boarders, including poet Richard Burton, and managed frequent dining and social activities. The club building was demolished in 1998.

CIVIC LEAGUE. In 1898, civic-minded members of the Woman's Club rented two rooms in an area known as "the swamp" (Englewood Avenue and Van Brunt Street) to start a day nursery. Their annual budget was $100 and more than 2,000 children attended the first year. The project expanded and soon they moved to this house at 32 North Dean. There were clubs and classes for women and children. Sewing school for girls over six was 1¢ per week; cooking, basketry, singing, and night school cost 5¢ per week.

ST. MICHAEL'S VILLA, 1889. The Sisters of St. Joseph of Newark erected a building on the crest of the Palisades to train and house women domestics, and to give working women a vacation retreat (for only $3 a week). With accommodations for 200 girls and only six sisters to do the work, it soon was impractical. The building then became a Novitiate and St. Joseph's Home for Boys. It burned in 1953.

43

CARPENTER'S QUARRY. During the 1700s and early 1800s fragments of Palisade rock were used for ballast in vessels. Later quarries opened and the rock was used for paving New York City streets. During the 1840s, Palisades "blue trap" built New Orleans' breakwaters. After the Civil War, excessive dynamite use threatened the actual cliff front. Elizabeth Veremilye formed a "Save the Palisades" movement, and by 1900, quarrying ended.

Cliff Hall, Englewood Cliffs, N. J.

CLIFF HALL C. 1895. The Englewood Cliffs Mayor and Council met in this large dance hall at 2 Seventh Street. The first ordinance passed was to prevent horses, goats, and other animals from running at large. Other early problems included proper observation of the Sabbath, fast riding and racing, and improper bathing attire. It seems some people liked to bathe nude in the Hudson! Cliff Hall also served as a Grand Opera House.

EARLY POLICE. In 1851, 22 voters formed a volunteer "Society for the Protection and Maintenance of Good Order" and used a single building as a police-fire station, lock-up, and courtroom. In 1869, there were "exempt members" who paid dues but performed no police functions and "marshals" who could be fined $20 for refusing to provide protection, but had no authority in civil litigation. In 1873, James A. Terhune was elected police chief. He hired five men who combatted public drunkenness, unmuzzled dogs, stolen pigeons, and wayward goats.

ENGLEWOOD'S FIRST FIREMEN. In 1887, Donald Mackay led the spontaneous bucket brigade that tried to save the Athenaeum; there were hydrants, but no hose. By 1888, Englewood had a volunteer association, a horse-drawn cart, fire truck, and a building on Van Brunt. Chief Jacob Ulrich and Assistant Emile Ruch hold speaking trumpets; Police Chief Terhune is top right. The volunteer crew assembled at the bell, rushed horses from nearby stables, and if the emergency was uphill, jumped off to push.

JOHN AND LETITIA SCOTT BROWN.
John, born in Bergen County in 1854, married Letitia Scott, a Native American of the Iroquois Nation from Hamilton, Canada in 1878. They moved to Englewood the next year and in 1894 built on Hirliman Road near Green Street. Self-employed, John cut and sold lumber and operated a successful cesspool business. They had 11 children; many of their descendants still live in Englewood.

ADALINE W. STERLING. In 1884, Adaline and Henriette Sawtelle organized a women's exchange (open until 1960) where gentlewomen could sell their handiwork and foodstuffs. Adaline was president of the Women's Club when it fought to save the Palisades in 1895. She was the first woman president of the school board in 1897. When the board was challenged, the New Jersey Supreme Court ruled in her favor. "The Book of Englewood," written by Miss Sterling in 1922, has been the fascinating major source for this book.

81 LINCOLN STREET C. 1876. This stone Victorian Gothic, one of three homes owned by the Homans family on a large plot, was bought in 1912 by George Graham. Treasurer of a hardware company, Graham was active in WW I fund drives, the Depot Park Committee, and was a Home Guard in the Englewood Rifle Club's motorcycle machine gun battery unit, the first of its kind in the U.S. The building is currently the admissions office of Dwight Englewood School.

BRINCKERHOFF HOUSE, 156 SHERWOOD AVENUE. Built as the Sherwood House in 1877, and renamed the Brinckerhoff House in 1911, it was made of coursed rubble brownstone in the Stick Style with some Gothic Revival elements. The date stone is the keystone of the first-story window. The Brinckerhoff family was large; it is rumored that the nickname for Palisade Avenue, "the seven sisters hill," refers not to the seven-stepped hill but to the seven Brinckerhoff sisters.

BANKS COFFIN HOUSE, 1890. Col. W. Henry Banks came to Englewood in 1867 and purchased Nathan T. Johnson's wooden "first house in the woods of the Palisades" framed in Boston and brought by schooner. When it burned, Banks built this stone French Country mansion. Banks was in the army, in the import business, founded the Field Club, the gas company, Citizen's National Bank, and held public office.

ACTORS FUND HOME, 155 W. HUDSON. In 1927, the Fund bought millionaire Hetty Green's 6-acre country estate and remodeled her Stanford White house as a retirement home for aging actors. Enrico Caruso donated a grand piano. The men had their billiard room; the women had their own Gay Nineties sanctuary with pink tufted sofas and small marble-topped tables on which tea was served every afternoon. In 1961, the present home replaced the above structure and a nursing home was added in 1985.

KLUGE ESTATE, "GREYSTONE," C. 1912, SOUTH HILLS. The estate employed a myriad of servants including an English riding master. Mrs. Kluge and her husband entertained Max Schmeling, Prince Matchabelli, Alfred Knopf, and Feodor Chaliapin. Landscaping included a pool, a sunken garden with a small Greek temple, and a deer park. The south porch had a hand painted ceiling dotted with tiny lights to resemble twinkling stars. Because drinks were served here, it was known as "souse porch."

THE ELKS CLUB. This club was built to give downtown businessmen a place to eat lunch. At the November 30, 1912 dedication, a huge elk's head was presented by Malcolm Mackay in honor of his father. Across Bennett Road the famed West Side Ball Park hosted games, the annual circus, and Christmas caroling. Today this Colonial Revival building is home to Ideal Lodge Of Elks No. 470 and Ideal Temple No. 290.

BATES HOUSE C. 1910. The Bates family built this cut brownstone house in an apple orchard on the north side of Hudson Avenue and Orchard Street. It had an elevator and a homemade grandfather clock. The dining room was paneled with beautiful beveled wood taken from old phone booths. An extensive basement was used for scientific experiments, and several outbuildings housed repair shops.

BLIZZARD OF 1888. The Bates family had fun in the snow, but the blizzard blocked roads and obstructed trains, telephones, and telegraph communication. Englewood township elections were held over from March 13 until April 10. Only two women made it to St. Paul's Church for Sunday services—no man braved the weather. Enthusiasts bobsledded from Woodland Avenue to William Street through to Tenafly Road.

ALICE BATES. She reminisced that the girls went to both Miss Gerrish's School and to public school, where they were never reprimanded because their father was on the school board. They enjoyed croquet, tennis, joy rides to Hackensack for dances, and outings on the Palisades.

THE BATES FAMILY. Shown on their Hudson Avenue porch, the family moved to Englewood from Cincinnati. Charles J. Bates trained at Annapolis and Rensselaer Polytechnic as an engineer. He built bridges and worked on his own inventions. The Bates had six children, among them are Mab, Alice, and George. George owned a Lincoln-Franklin automobile agency on Hudson Avenue.

51

ST. PAUL'S EPISCOPAL CHURCH
ENGLEWOOD, N.J.

ST. PAUL'S. In 1865, an Episcopalian group that met at the Van Brunt Street Armory made plans to build a church. Rev. Ozi Whitaker, a missionary from Nevada, who was visiting his sister, stayed on to guide the group and became its first rector. In 1900, the congregation, hard pressed for space, replaced its modest building with this Tudor-Gothic structure. English Ivy transplanted from Canterbury Cathedral in England climbed its walls.

VIEW IN BROOKSIDE CEMETERY,
ENGLEWOOD N.J.

BROOKSIDE CEMETERY. The land, purchased in 1876, is located between two streams feeding an icehouse that closed when residents thought the water impure. In 1880, more land was bought and 1750 trees planted. Many Englewood notables are buried here, some with full military honors. Moses Springer, temperance leader and undertaker, was the first superintendent of Brookside.

52

ST. JOHN'S CHURCH C. 1887. So that congregants living far from St. Paul's could worship in their own neighborhood, Mrs. Walter Phelps gifted a mission church at Grand Avenue and Nordhoff. William Burdett, a devoted lay worker, led the congregation. Through the years the rectorate never placed a full time minister there. Membership dwindled after WW II and the church closed in 1979. The building still stands.

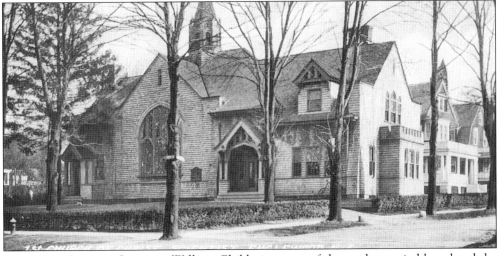

CHRISTIAN SCIENCE CHURCH. William Childs, inventor of the modern switchboard and the man who introduced a telephone exchange system to Englewood, was healed through Christian Science. Interested friends and neighbors formed a group that met at his Woodland home in 1898 and later rented a storefront. In 1901, they built at Engle and Spring Streets. During WW I, the congregation worked at the Christian Science Welfare House bordering Camp Merritt. A church member recalls bringing her garden hose to offer drinks to soldiers marching off to war.

DWIGHT CHAPEL C. 1883, W. PALISADE AVENUE. The First Presbyterian Church held the deed to this building and designated it for community use. The first African-American congregation in Englewood, a mission project of the church, met here. Eventually the building was moved up Palisade Avenue with a large parade to Lafayette Street and Tenafly Road where it stands today. Bethany Presbyterian was built with the proceeds on the original site.

THE FIRST WEST SIDE PRESBYTERIAN. Dwight Chapel was purchased by Union Chapel members who originally worshipped in Kursteiner's schoolhouse. The building was raised onto a stone foundation and became West Side Church. Under Rev. Charles Smith they expanded and also bought the West Side Athletic Field across the street, inviting the community to enjoy local competitions and caroling under the pine trees.

OLD SHILOH. Shiloh African Methodist Episcopal Zion Church was organized in 1891 under the leadership of Louis Mason. It was first located on the corner of Van Brunt and Palisade Avenue, then moved to School Street, to Englewood Avenue, and finally to William Street where the church pictured was erected in 1910. In 1977 under the pastorate of Rev. Alfred E. Garnette, a modern edifice was built on the same premises.

FIRST BAPTIST CHURCH OF ENGLEWOOD. Englewood's first African-American Baptist congregation first met under a tent in 1873, then at a house, and finally at 61 William Street where the building shown was erected. In 1969, the congregation built a new modern building on Englewood Avenue at Oak Street under the pastorate of Reverend J. Isiah Goodman. This church has been a central meeting place for Englewood's African-American community.

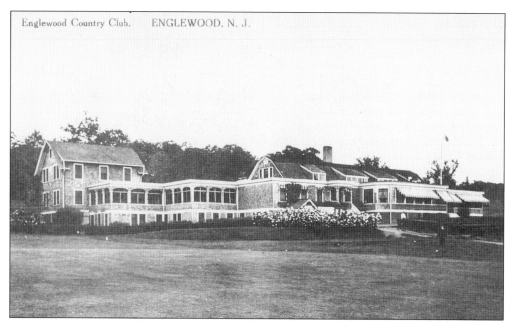

Englewood Country Club. ENGLEWOOD, N. J.

ENGLEWOOD GOLF CLUB C. 1895. The Niblick Realty Company developed a nine-hole course in the South Hills of the Second Ward. Pink-coated members and their guests played golf among the fruit trees. The course tested the Sunday blue laws. When prominent citizens allowed themselves to be arrested, the case was promptly dismissed and "Sunday golfers live unmolested in our midst." The course was expanded to 18 holes and in 1909 hosted the Men's US Open Golf Championship. The movie industry used the grounds as a back lot.

PALISADES TEA PARTY. The Bates sisters and their friends, like many local residents, enjoyed regular jaunts to the Cliffs for health and relaxation. The first record of anyone falling off the cliffs and surviving was in 1870 when a young man named Anderson, picnicking with friends, fell 250 feet. Rescued after 2 1/2 hours, he was carried to the nearby Coe mansion and treated by Dr. Currie.

PIONEER BASEBALL CLUB C. 1885. These "nine stalwart youths, well trained, clean players" played at a lot on the corner of John Street and Tenafly Road. The first Englewood baseball club, organized in 1860 with 29 members included J.W. Jones, Rev. Dwight, J.A. Humphrey, the Homans brothers, James W. Deuel, Francis Howland, Nathan T. Johnson, and Joseph Stagg. They played near the Liberty Pole.

Field Club House, Englewood, N. J.

Dear Edith, Lit has just had her nose broke and she is quite mad about it. affectionately Ethel Blaubeuho

August 31, 1906

FIELD CLUB BUILDING #2. In 1887, a group of restless young men proposed to form a club "in the interest of outdoor sport . . . to promote recreation and social intercourse among its members." The first modest clubhouse was moved next to the pond to become the skate house. Families came through the surrounding woods to skate between blades of winter grass on the boggy dammed-up brook.

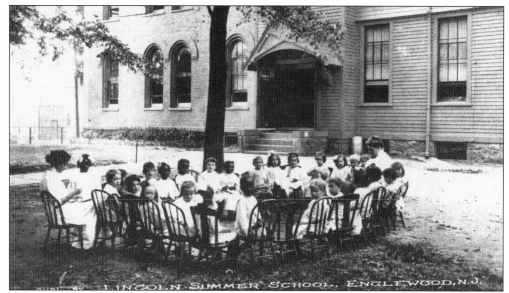

LINCOLN SCHOOL C. 1916, ENGLEWOOD AVENUE. In 1867, New Jersey mandated free public education for all children ages five to 18. In 1868, Englewood subscribed $3,000, added the state's $1,000, and built Lincoln (small brick section). In 1884, Lincoln was enlarged to include the School for Colored Children, and four years later, a large frame addition was built to house its 1,000 pupils. Lincoln became Englewood's first social center in 1911 with classes in handwork and folk dancing. It burned in 1917; the present structure was built the next year.

ENGLEWOOD SCHOOL FOR BOYS. This school opposite the Field Club c. 1891 featured systematic military drills and a college preparatory curriculum. In 1916, Englewood's Mayor Blake, endorsed by the Englewood Rifle Club, urged military training in the public schools as well. The city of Englewood kept a census of college men, and each year held a dinner in their honor. In 1923, there were 265 graduates of 32 different universities.

STUDENTS OF SMITH'S PRIVATE SCHOOL, 1886. Principal W.W. Smith with moustache, seated center, is surrounded by students including Sheppard Homans, Seward Prosser, Vernon Monroe, Dan Platt, Smith Homans, and Cameron Blaikie. Many became important men in Englewood. The school, located in the Athenaeum, closed when the building burned. Mr. Smith then became active in the military school.

NORDHOFF SCHOOL. This school opened in 1895 while still unfinished. Miss Elizabeth Bennett and Mrs. Isabella Arrow "carried pupils through the first four grades." The Nordhoff area was originally called Walton. The name changed when William Walter Phelps named its post office after a friend. Nordhoff residents overwhelmingly voted with pride to join the new city of Englewood in 1899 to the prejudice of Ridgefield Township.

DWIGHT SCHOOL, 1899. This school was founded by Euphemia Creighton and Ellen Farrar as a private home and day school for girls. Although Dwight was a common Englewood name, they named this school in honor of the president of Yale, Rev. Timothy Dwight, whose education philosophy they admired. They believed in small classes and inspiring teaching. By 1925, the founders turned the school over to a board of trustees as a nonprofit organization dedicated to the superior education of young girls.

UNDERCLIFF SCHOOL C. 1876. In 1867, 26 school children who lived in Undercliff attended "the swamp school" (Lincoln). This trek shortened many a school career. Wm. Dana financed the Undercliff School, mostly attended by young children, with the older students still trudging to Lincoln. In 1896 teacher Margaret Von Wagoner was paid $45 per month during the season. Later, artist Van Deering Perrine lived here with his Japanese houseboy.

THE ICEHOUSE AT CRYSTAL LAKE, NORDHOFF C. 1890. Crystal Lake froze in the winter and was a popular destination for ice-skating. It was also the source for blocks of ice, cut and stored in the icehouse. The Hygeia Company, advertising more healthful properties for its artificial ice, competed vigorously for trade. In 1850 this area was subject to a "pearlers rush" when valuable pearls were found in the local freshwater mussels of Overpeck Creek's tributaries.

BARRET, PALMER, AND NEAL DYEWORKS, CEDAR LANE, NORDHOFF. The company used Overpeck Creek water to dye and finish fabrics. It was the former site of Tide Water Mill where scows and tugs came up creek to get logs. The tide was retained in flooded meadows and channeled to turn the mill wheel. By 1920, Englewood manufacturing earned $1,119,000 per annum. The NJ Paper Tube Works near the railroad station produced one carload of ice-cream soda straws each month. Pottery clay was mined on Mary Street.

ENGLEWOOD'S EARLY MAYORS. Pictured above from left to right are: (seated) Mayors Elbert A. Brinckerhoff (1899–1901) and Daniel A. Currie (1901–1903); (standing) Dan Fellows Platt (1904–1905), Donald Mackay (1906–1909), and James A.C. Johnson (1910, resigned to become state senator). Englewood township, with a population of 5,443 minus the newly incorporated boroughs of Englewood Cliffs and Teaneck, formed a de facto city in 1897. Englewood was legally incorporated as a city on March 21, 1899. It was the first city in Bergen County.

DR. DANIEL CURRIE. Born on a farm in Searsville, New York, Dr. Currie followed his prominent Scottish grandfather into medicine. After medical school in Buffalo, he apprenticed two years in Edinburgh and moved to Englewood in 1872. He became a widely popular physician and a local hero. He was elected mayor three times on the Democratic ticket, besting illustrious Republican opponents. In 1898 he volunteered in the Spanish-American War.

Three

THE BEDROOM OF WALL STREET

During the first third of the 20th century, "the Queen City of the Palisades" underwent many changes: the car superceded the horse; the ferry and streetcar made travel to New York more affordable; the city developed a social consciousness; the hospitals, library, and schools were refined and enlarged; social service agencies developed new programs; people from other countries or other regions of our country came here for economic betterment; and citizens banded together to develop working institutions. Homes ranged from a "lordly castle at $100,000 to a roomy cottage at $2,000." Finally with the coming of the bridge, there was easy transportation to New York City, generating new sub-divisions and an increasingly diverse population, as Englewood changed from a haven for the wealthy to a unique suburb.

FIREMEN'S CONVENTION PARADE, 1904. The firemen assembled at the Lyceum for dinner and speeches, then had a grand parade through much of the city. The parade included a march to the Highwood Fire Station, then south to the Nordhoff fire station, then back to the Lyceum. This view looking west on Palisade Avenue pictures some houses later moved for new stores. Buildings were often moved due to the scarcity and expense of building materials.

MOVING CITY HALL. The first city hall was built *c.* 1860 on Palisade Avenue near the railroad tracks as a hotel pub by Joseph Stagg and managed by John Ackerman. Railroad directors met here at Stagg's (also known as Ackerman's) before its use as the city hall (*c.* 1899). Englewood took title to the building in 1909. Scene of a gala celebration at the end of WW I, it was moved down Van Brunt to Englewood Avenue in 1921, and demolished in 1974.

CITY HALL, 1923. A new building with expanded quarters and a new jail (the old one had been condemned in 1921) had been needed for years. After much controversy, the old site of city hall was used; quicksand was discovered while digging the foundation, but construction continued. The new city hall, a classical building with an attractive interior, was dedicated July 4, 1923, with elaborate ceremonies and a parade.

SCHWARTZ NUTZHORN GROCERY. In 1893 Adolph Nutzhorn and his cousin Frederick paid the Seemans $425 for an interest in and the contents of a grocery (10 pounds lemon peel, 40 pounds codfish, 3 pots chicken). The third owner of the store on the north side of Palisade Avenue and the three-story brick building housing it was Schwartz, "uncle" to Adolph's future bride Emma. Nutzhorn traded as the Bergen County Tea Company and went out of business after over-extending credit to his customers.

NUTZHORN LUNCH WAGON. In 1907 Adolph leased a "new or second hand lunch wagon" for "$60 down and $60 a month for five years" and located it where heavy farm wagons would rest before or after traversing Palisade Avenue. Lighter carts guided by a wire up or down the hill were introduced. The lunch wagon failed. Adolph then opened a milk delivery business in 1909. He eventually became a full-time Lutheran pastor.

BUTCHER SHOP, 63 N. DEAN. Charles Weidig came to New York City from Germany in 1860 and opened a smoking and curing business. He traveled Bergen County buying hogs and cattle and herding them back for slaughter via the 42nd St. Ferry. Later his son Philip M. opened a butcher shop in Stagg's Hall on Palisade Avenue, moved up to the DeMott Building for 25 years, and finally settled here with his own son Philip E.

WEIDIG BROTHERS. Philip E. and Joseph took over from their father in 1916. Two years earlier, Philip E. had met his wife, Elsa, cook at the J.S. Coffin House, while making deliveries. In those days everything was fresh; whole animals were delivered for butchering, carcasses arrived via refrigerated train car from Chicago, and the A&P was "just a tiny hole in the wall" near the monument.

WEIDIG HOME, 187 JOHN ST. C. 1910. Pictured here are Hulda, Philip M.'s third wife, and children. Up the street was Jake Banta's ice business, then Dan Platt's first home with acres of fields and horses, and, behind the Platts, Andrew Demarest's carpentry barns. Philip E. and Elsa lived at 157 John Street. Aside from being very active in the business and raising children, Elsa, an opera buff, had a close friendship with Wagnerian tenor Lauritz Melchior. In 1978 at age 84 and still going strong, she finished the 5,000-meter run in Englewood's Senior Marathon.

ENGLEWOOD'S FIRST AUTO DELIVERY TRUCK. A one-cylinder Cadillac driven in 1906 by Philip E. Weidig served as the first auto delivery truck. Weidig's store clerk, John Daley, still delivered by horse and wagon. Peoples Market had a thriving business with the Hill mansions. Prime ribs were 25¢ a pound, porterhouse 32¢, and French chops 25¢. Specialties were Canada mutton and Southdown lamb. The market's telephone number was "8."

THE FIRST CAR IN ENGLEWOOD. The car was purchased in 1902 by E.H. Lyon "who took Palisade hill at greater speed than a horse could make." In 1909 the city authorized the Englewood Automotive Club to experiment with different road surfaces on Dana Place. Lyon privately defrayed all expenses. In 1905 Laura Drake Smith, the first Englewood woman to drive a car, drove her Chalmers to Brooklyn and back in two days. She was stopped for speeding by a policeman on a bicycle.

GEORGE R. WEST C. 1920S. Shown here dressed in his chauffeur outfit with his latest car on West Palisade Avenue, West, an entrepreneur, operated a garage on South Van Brunt Street. He later owned and operated the Fort Lee Riding Academy where he boarded and trained horses. George West married Ruth Brown, and they lived on Reade Street where they raised three children.

ROBERT LIVINGSTON. This store opened on Palisade Avenue sometime before 1900 selling high-class stationery, newspapers, magazines, Kodak, and smokers' supplies. Later, Livingston opened branches at Dean Street and at Depot Square. In 1899 F.W. Bergendahl was arrested for selling ice cream on Sunday at his Palisade Avenue parlor, but was found not guilty. By 1913 Avenue shops included three beer bottlers, a cigar maker, and two Chinese laundries.

PALISADE AVENUE. National Beef Company opened at 11 E. Palisade Avenue by 1922. Robert Livingston was on the corner. Other Avenue stores included "Doc" Dincin's, the first drugstore to sell an African-American published newspaper, *The Age*; Taylor's Cigar Store, owned by a Russian-born Jew from Dublin, where the Sons of Irish Freedom hung out; Siciliano Brothers, hat cleaners; a harness maker; and four shoemakers. There were ten shoemakers operating in Englewood in 1922.

LIBRARY, PALISADE AVENUE. Englewood's first library in the Lyceum belonged solely to its subscribers, who paid dues of $5. Life membership subscriptions of $200 raised $3,400 for books. Founder Rev. Daniel Wise lamented "more books borrowed address the imagination than the development of intellect and morality." In 1901 Donald Mackay donated the Ainsworth house next door, stipulating taxation for its maintenance. The Englewood Free Public Library opened there with 7,000 volumes. Miss Harriet Prosser was librarian.

CARNEGIE LIBRARY. The library was designed by the important architectural firm of Boring and Tilton and built under Carnegie Corporation provisions in 1914 after moving the Mackay library building to the back of the lot. It had 14,287 books and a membership of 2,424. In 1921 children's story hour started, and hundreds of children came to listen. By 1929 a new addition housed a children's room and the library contained almost 30,000 books.

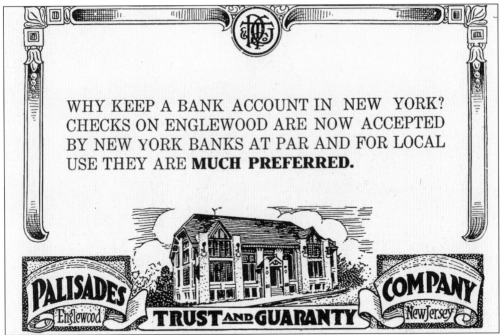

WHY KEEP A BANK ACCOUNT IN NEW YORK?
CHECKS ON ENGLEWOOD ARE NOW ACCEPTED
BY NEW YORK BANKS AT PAR AND FOR LOCAL
USE THEY ARE **MUCH PREFERRED.**

PALISADES
Englewood
TRUST AND GUARANTY
COMPANY
New Jersey

PALISADES TRUST AND GUARANTY COMPANY, PARK PLACE. This Tudor-style building was designed in 1906 by famous architect and Englewood resident Aymar Embury II. It was incorporated in 1902 with offices in the Bergen Building. Original incorporators include Allison, Currie, Platt, Coe, A. Westervelt, O.D. Smith, and its first president, Abram DeRonde. Jacob Demarest was teller. The nearby Englewood Mutual Loan and Building Association (1887) invested in local first mortgages and helped members buy homes.

BERGEN BUILDING. This structure on the corner of Engle and Bergen Streets, burned March 10, 1911. High winds and low water pressure contributed to a $40,000 loss. In 1900, the Bergen County Gas & Electric company (est. 1869) built the Bergen Building, Englewood's first modern apartment house, with six upstairs apartments "equipped for housekeeping." The first story held stores, its own and others' offices, including the telephone exchange (est. 1886 with 60 subscribers), and the Sewerage Association (est. 1887).

71

ROOSEVELT SCHOOL, BROAD AVENUE. Teddy Roosevelt Jr. spoke at the 1926 dedication, along with Dwight Morrow, Winton White, and Mayor Thomson. Early Georgian in design, the school had a 500-seat auditorium with a motion picture machine, a gymnasium with a spectator gallery, a manual training shop, and a courtyard. The charming double kindergarten room had low seats by a large fireplace. It is now a condominium.

LINCOLN CLASSROOM. In November 1918 the new Lincoln School opened with principal Miss Lillian Hover and Mayor McKenna speaking. William Tierney led the audience in community singing. This lovely classroom now contains the art and music rooms. Decorative tiles surround the fireplace and the water fountains. The border has nursery rhyme pictures. A dental chair for pupil checkups was located in an upstairs office.

ELISABETH MORROW SCHOOL. The school was founded in 1930 as The Little School by Elisabeth Morrow and Constance Chilton in a farmhouse on East Linden Avenue. They began with 34 students, ages 18 months to five years. Chilton and Morrow, Smith College graduates, had an interest in early education and an educational philosophy that "preserved the best of the old and adapted the best of the new."

SONGS AND MOVEMENT. At Elisabeth Morrow School children learned "by doing rather than by bookwork alone." It grew from a nursery school to include the upper elementary grades. Tradition played an important role in the educational experience. As they entered school each morning, the boys, dressed in jackets and ties, and the girls, in skirts or dresses, politely shook hands with a staff greeter at the door. In the mid-1930s the school moved to the Morrow estate on Next Day Hill, where it stands today.

DWIGHT SCHOOL SENIOR CLASS, 1902. A combination of rigorous education, fine social life, and social conscience defined the school. This nine member graduating class went to college: Vassar, Smith, and Wellesley. To assure the propriety of their costume, the dresses the girls were to wear to school dances were preapproved by Misses Creighton and Farrar. In 1917 two seniors bought a truck and took it to France to distribute food and clothing to war-torn families.

DWIGHT CLASSROOM, 1904. Students studied Latin, French, and ancient history, as well as traditional subjects, and made frequent trips to the Metropolitan Opera, Carnegie Hall, and New York City museums. The school also sponsored study trips to Europe in the summer. The Englewood School for Boys (no relation to previous schools so named), which was founded in 1928 as a local preparatory school, merged with Dwight School in 1973.

74

DWIGHT SCHOOL BOARDERS, 1925. Although some were day students, most of the girls were boarding students who lived in Dwight House, the Cottage, and also on the second floor of the gym, where they enjoyed slumber parties on the roof. Here they are playing the ukulele while sitting on Miss Creighton's car, with her dog.

KLUGE FAMILY, 1923. Alexandra and Thais graduated from Dwight, but during WW I, unwelcome at their private school because their parents were suspected enemy aliens, the children attended Lincoln where they made only one friend—a Japanese boy. Pictured on South Porch are Emile Kluge of Germany, president of E.H. Kluge Weaving Company; his wife Olga de Moravsky, descended from Russian nobility, active in the Russian Orthodox Church in New York City, and president of the Russian-American War Relief Society; and their children, Alexandra, who wrote an autobiography "Princess in Paradise," Thais, Emile, and Serge.

LIBERTY SCHOOL. The school, the first public building authorized by the new city and designed by Davis, McGrath and Kiesling, was built in 1902 at Liberty Square. To make room, Liberty Road was relocated one block north. The elementary school also housed several high school classes on the second floor. Increased attendance necessitated symmetrical additions to the Jacobean Revival core (1913 and 1927), the latter designed by Lawrence Licht. This oldest surviving public school building is currently used for administration.

FRANKLIN SCHOOL, ENGLE STREET. Built on the site of the current Englewood Library and dedicated in 1907, the school was named in honor of Benjamin Franklin. The building housed elementary grades but the upper floor also served as the Englewood High School until 1917. At that time, high school classes were also held across town at Liberty. In 1933, the upper floors were connected to the next-door junior high school by a passageway.

FRANKLIN CLASS. Shown here is a group of Franklin students sometime before the last high school class graduated in 1917. In 1905, evening school was inaugurated for students over 14 who could not attend during the day. The first week, 94 students attended. In 1906 when retaining instructors was a problem, Adaline Sterling called attention to their scant average salaries of $600 per year.

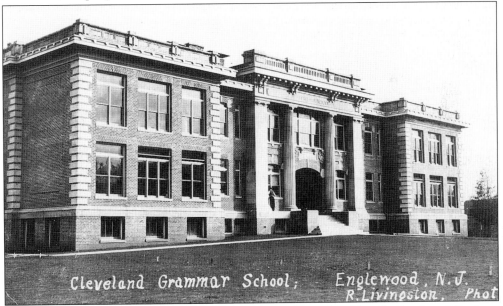

Cleveland Grammar School, Englewood, N.J.
R. Livingston, Phot

CLEVELAND SCHOOL. Built in 1910, the school was located at Tenafly Road and Durie to replace Highwood, the inconvenient Orchard Street structure known as School #2. Students from Englewood's northwest area attended. At its gala dedication, Charles Bates, on behalf of the Highwood Association, presented a large crayon portrait of President Grover Cleveland, and the principal, Miss Sue C. Kerr, delivered a ringing patriotic address.

St. Cecilia High School. Children play in front of the English Gothic-style school built in 1924. Raphael Hume designed this first Catholic High School in Bergen County to contain a 1,000-seat auditorium and a gymnasium with side galleries seating 1,000. The gym was also used for dances and card parties. The football banquet was held in the cafeteria. Students from 24 towns attended in 1928.

Cheerleaders, 1929. These stylish young ladies who chanted "ala garu, garu, garrah" were St. Cecilia High School cheerleaders. The high school has a rich tradition of good sports teams. In 1929 they had baseball, football, and boys' and girls' basketball teams. The boys' head coach was All-American fullback Louis "Red" Gebhard. In the 1940s, when not teaching chemistry or Latin, Vince Lombardi coached football.

78

EHS Girls Basketball Team 1907–08. This team won the first championship of any team (boys or girls) in Englewood High School history. They won seven and lost two, including outscoring Paterson 22-3, Hackensack 25-4, and Nutley 31-10. Pictured here from left to right are: (front row) Tierney, Van Janot, and Marshall; (back row) Cole, Tuttle, Macalister, and Hill.

Engle Street School. Formerly the site of the Englewood House, the school was built in 1910 in the English Renaissance Revival style with a large auditorium, gymnasium with a balcony, and a controversial swimming pool. This new high school became a receiving center for students from Tenafly (until 1922), Edgewater, Ridgefield, Oradell, and Harrington Park. In 1933 it became the junior high. Now it is the Renaissance Center office building.

ENGLEWOOD HIGH SCHOOL TRACK TEAM, 1909. Brotherton, Aggus, Caswell, Reeve, Green, Fenno, and G. Vossler won trophies in league meets and the Penn relays. Winton White was an early track coach and later high school principal and superintendent. He convinced the public to build a new athletic field. Eight hundred school children pledged their pennies toward the $50,000 cost. The field, later Winton White Stadium, was dedicated in 1923.

EHS BASKETBALL TEAM, 1925–26. The team had a record of ten wins and eight losses, with two wins each over rivals Leonia and Hackensack. They defeated Hackensack 26-17 and 27-20. "Bim" Bering led the team in scoring with over 115 points for the season. Coach Hurlburt had two of the best guards in the league in Elzy Campball and Evie Levinsohn. Other players included Jack Miller, Beano Rivara, and George Doyle.

DWIGHT MORROW HIGH SCHOOL DEDICATION, 1933. State Commissioner of Education Charles Elliott was the main speaker, Mayor Kitchel spoke, School Board President Thomas Cox pronounced the dedication, and School Superintendent Winton White opened the ceremony. The ceremonial keys were accepted by Mrs. Dwight (Elizabeth) Morrow. In 1931 she put mortar on the first brick and assisted her daughters Anne and Elisabeth in laying the cornerstone.

DWIGHT MORROW HIGH SCHOOL. One of the most beautiful public high schools in the state, this 37-acre campus school with a distinctive 120-foot bell tower was designed by Lawrence Licht and completed in 1932. Seminar rooms patterned after Oxford were wood paneled and hung with replicas of old masters. The school was named for statesman, financier, and local activist Dwight Morrow, who in 1911 at the dedication of Cleveland School, gave a speech entitled "The Values of Public Education."

TILLOTSON'S C. 1920. Ebon Winton founded the *Englewood Times* in 1874 in the old Livingston Building. In 1879, Joseph A Tillotson and Henry M. Lichtenberg opened *The Standard* in the DeMott Building. In 1890, proprietor and editor Joseph Tillotson published the first issue of the weekly *Englewood Press*. The *Press* was at first editorially Republican but eventually became non-partisan. In 1900, Tillotson began publishing address/occupation books. In 1911, the *Press's* second place of business in the Van Horne building burned. It was rebuilt on the same site.

TROLLEY. From Ferry Plaza in Pleasant Valley, now Edgewater (a ten-minute ferry ride from New York City costing 5¢), the electric railway zig-zagged along the Palisades, then followed broad suburban avenues to Englewood. There, the private right of way ran on Dean Street from Nordhoff to Palisade Avenue (1896). By 1900 the line extended to Highwood and by 1911 to Tenafly. The trip took 35 minutes and cost 10¢. The last trolley ran in 1926.

ENGLEWOOD THEATER. This local vaudeville house on East Palisade Avenue once awarded a belled cow on prize night. During WW I Manager Samuel Perry distributed free tickets through the Soldier's Club. The earliest movies cost a nickel at the Lyceum. The Bijou opened July 20, 1909 charging 10¢ (children 5¢) for a matinee and changed the bill of "moving pictures and illustrated songs" daily. The Plaza Theater (now John Harms) on North Van Brunt Street opened November 22, 1926 showing Harry Langdon in *Strong Man* and vaudeville shows.

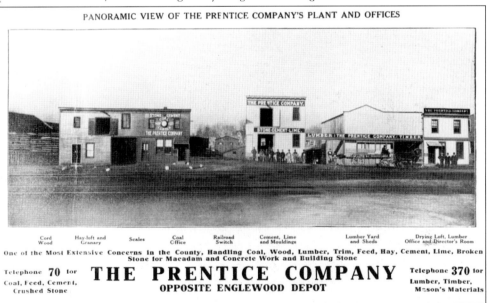

PRENTICE COMPANY, 1911. Many businesses clustered near the railroad depots, crowding out park land. Earlier, when most streets in town were treeless, the little park surrounded by a railing near the depot had shady elms and maples, as well as a pond where people picnicked, talked politics, and tethered their horses. Later this park was known as Veterans Memorial or Colonel Moore Park. It is now called Depot Park. Moore, an "outstanding soldier and citizen," and 1924 mayor, is the only citizen honored by a local monument.

ENGLEWOOD HOSPITAL. Only 11 years after admitting its first patient the hospital had expanded to the point where its bed capacity doubled. In 1923 under Seward Prosser, $1,064,000 was raised to build and equip a new facility. The new Renaissance-Revival hospital building which officially opened in the fall of 1925 is now the East Wing, and its private pavilion has been converted to a maternity department.

ENGLEWOOD FLOWER DANCE AT THE LYCEUM, 1889. The Kirmess (folk dancing), an Englewood Hospital fund-raiser, included Highland reels, and Japanese and Gypsy dances. In 1923, Adolph Zukor wrote and Morrow, Prosser, and Lamont acted in an Englewood Hospital movie. Englewood supported drives for Near-East relief, Jewish relief, Chinese famines, colleges, charities, and WW I with fairs, carnivals, boxing exhibitions with "Gentleman" Jim Corbett, baseball games, and charity balls.

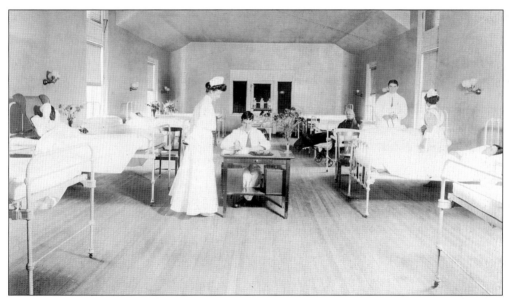

NURSING WARD. Despite good orderlies, the hospital was not immaculate enough to satisfy the nursing students, so each week they took turns scrubbing the floors of the wards. In addition, concerned about the aesthetics of the wards, they hung lace curtains.

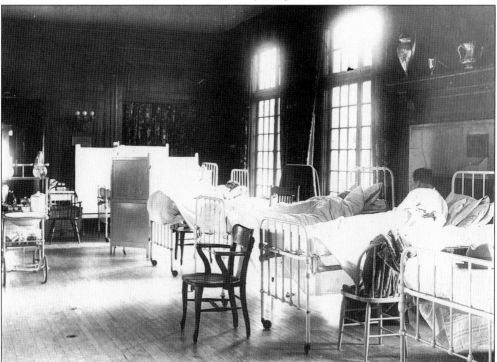

SPANISH INFLUENZA EPIDEMIC. Without antibiotics, this virus brought disaster in 1918. Twenty million people died worldwide. The Field Club, as pictured, turned over all its facilities to the Red Cross and Englewood Hospital for an emergency ward. Almost overnight it was adequately equipped. Club members volunteered full time to relieve overburdened hospital staff and contributed or funded supplies.

ENGLEWOOD INN. During WW I, when the need for trained nurses escalated, 18 nurses from Englewood served, but the school could not train more until they obtained a residence facility. Finally, Mrs. W.L. Pierce Sr. donated this property, which had been the Englewood School for Boys and was being used as an inn, to the hospital for use as a nurses' residence.

EARLY AMBULANCE. In 1892, the first ambulance was funded by a subscription drive started by the *Englewood Press*. In 1914, the nursing curriculum included lectures in skin, venereal and mental diseases, serum therapy, and anesthesia. Nurses rode the ambulances, mopped floors, and sometimes put in 16 hours on duty. In the postwar years, students were restricted to the grounds after 7 p.m., except for one night when they could stay out until 10.

FIRST PUBLIC HEALTH NURSES, 1925. Community nursing was deemed essential "affecting the life and health of the city" by the National Red Cross, the Social Service Federation, the Tuberculosis and Health Association, and Englewood Hospital. They cooperatively set up a plan with the hospital to run the program. All groups would contribute financially to the newly formed department.

LEAVING FOR A DAY OF HOME VISITS, 1931. Public health nurses did preventive instruction and limited emergency bedside care. They investigated conditions affecting infant mortality and, communicable diseases, inspection and supervision of midwives, and registration of unreported births. They taught basic hygiene and alerted clients to the dangers of self-medication, the use of patent medicines like Lydia Pinkham's Vegetable Compound, promises of "Colds Cured in a Day," and assorted faith cures.

RED CROSS. In August 1914, Mrs. George H. Payson gathered women to make surgical dressings for British war relief. Weekly, then daily, meetings were held at St. Paul's Church. When the United States entered the war in 1917, Red Cross workers met at the Grand Avenue Methodist Church. About 150 volunteers made dressings and received instruction in home nursing and first aid. Each woman was expected to pledge the maximum time possible.

THE BUNNIES SAYING GRACE, 1919. The Edgewater Creche, on Broad Avenue with buildings on 6 acres, was started in 1884 to take care of delicate children. Mrs. Donald Mackay donated one building, the gatehouse. Children of many different nationalities and religions, sent by 20 different agencies, were helped by the Creche, which also placed some of the children for adoption. The Creche was chiefly funded by voluntary contributions.

ROAD TO DYCKMAN FERRY. This zigzag road was built by the Palisades Road and Turnpike Company to service the Palisades Mountain House in the 1880s. In those days it was a toll road, charging 4¢ for a person on horseback, 6¢ for a horse and carriage. When the ferry was popular, the Sunday afternoon line of waiting cars would extend up the cliffs and down Palisade Avenue as far as Jones Road.

Dyckman Street Ferry from the Palisades   Englewood, N. J.

DYCKMAN STREET FERRY. The ferry opened in 1915 to accommodate automobiles crossing to the Englewood area. The old landing from the Palisades Mountain House was used as the first terminus. Later, after more landfill was created in part by dumping ashes from the ferry boilers, a new dock was built. The original fare was 3¢ per passenger, 30¢ for a roadster. Often the ferry was crowded with actors going to Fort Lee studios.

MᴄLᴏᴜɢʜʟɪɴ Wᴇᴅᴅɪɴɢ, 1924. Marie Hickey married John McLoughlin Sr. at St. Cecilia's Church; the best man was Edward O'Neill, son of the police chief. This wedding portrait was taken in front of Marie's mother's house at 124 Tenafly Road. Marie's father, Thomas Hickey, was a tinsmith (Hickey and Baker, Bergen Street), volunteer fireman, and the city's Poormaster, overseeing those citizens with unusual hardships.

Cʜʀɪsᴛᴇɴɪɴɢ Dᴀʏ. Grandparents Michael and Delia Noonan McLoughlin joined family members on John Street for Mary Helene's christening. Michael and Delia emigrated from Ireland before the turn of the century and met while working at the Hotel Astor. Delia's given name was Bridget, but in the United States this name had derogatory associations for Irish girls, so she became Delia.

Mary Helene McLoughlin, 1930. Mary, the oldest of five, poses on the running board of an Auburn at her John Street house. During the Depression her father John Sr. scrambled hard to find part-time work; he delivered holiday mail, worked for the WPA on the Lincoln Tunnel, shoveled snow for 50¢. When her parents managed a Catskills summer hotel, the family lived in a tent. Public Service hired John Sr. full time in 1939. Mary's brother, John Jr., still lives on John Street.

English Family, 1927. Whittie English came from North Carolina in 1927 and worked as a sandhog and in construction. His family includes wife Jennie (d.1930) and children Jennie, Whittie Jr., Josephine, and Hattie. Jennie, a nurse anesthesiologist, works with her sister Dr. Josephine English, an Ob-Gyn. Whittie Jr., a Tuskegee Airman, Englewood developer and builder, along with sister Hattie Harper work together in real estate.

DAVISON-LAMONT MANSION C. 1891. This mansion on Beech Road was built by Mann and McNeil for Henry P. Davison, who made Englewood famous as the bedroom of Wall Street. He and George Case founded Bankers Trust, enlisting Thomas Lamont, Seward Prosser, and Daniel Pomeroy. As partner in J.P.Morgan, he recruited Lamont and Dwight Morrow. Davison put Englewood Hospital on a sound financial footing. In 1912 Lamont bought the mansion. Morgan partner, and later chairman, Lamont represented the United States on international financial commissions, financed the *Saturday Review of Literature*, and served on the Board of Harvard University.

COE/POMEROY HOUSE, BEECH ROAD. This house was built in 1906 by Edward Coe, 1896 Englewood councilman and president of the Englewood Club. The brick and stucco tudor with half timbering designed by neighbor and architect Aymar Embury II was sold to Daniel Pomeroy, vice president of Bankers Trust, Republican National Committeeman, and Herbert Hoover's campaign manager. Pomeroy was also a naturalist, sportsman, trustee of the American Museum of Natural History, and member of the Eastman Expedition to British East Africa.

GLORIA CREST, 83 NORTH WOODLAND AVENUE, 1926. Count Stefan Poniatowski, one time heir to the Polish throne, made millions in the silk industry and built this opulent Italian style villa. His wife, Edythe (nee Von Stohn), landscaped the walled 5 acres with manicured trees and exotic gardens. Her diary details the sale of the house after the stock market crash. "Gloria Crest" refers to the location, not to Gloria Swanson's rumored tryst with Ambassador Joseph Kennedy at this villa.

THE MAXWELL UPSON MANSION, 320 MOUNTAIN ROAD, C. 1920. Considered the most imposing mansion in Englewood, this French chateau was designed by the architect of the Washington Cathedral. Upson, president of the Raymond Concrete Pile Company, admirer of Herbert Hoover, and Republican National Committeeman, supported every Englewood institution of his day. Upson willed hundreds of thousands of dollars to Englewood's hospital and public library.

PLATT HOUSE, BOOTH AVENUE, C. 1909. This Italianate Renaissance Revival house was designed by Davis McGrath and Kiessling. Dan Platt was an archeologist, art collector, mayor (1903), and 1912 Democratic convention delegate. He developed Hot Springs, Arkansas and owned hotels there. Platt's art collection was given to Princeton, Yale, and the National Gallery. His wife, author and tennis player Ethel Appleby Bliss Platt, led the Englewood suffragists as they organized as a separate branch of the Northern Valley Women's Political Union in 1914.

SCHAEFER RESIDENCE, 41 NORTH WOODLAND. This was the Tudor-style home of Eugene and Anna Schaefer. Schaefer, a chemist who founded Maywood Chemicals, had an outstanding collection of early art glass objects, now housed at the Newark Museum. Many Englewood residents were concerned with beautiful landscaping. Children would cross scraggly privet hedges to visit neighbors' formal gardens, including some planned by Frederick Law Olmstead, Englewood resident and designer of New York City's Central Park.

HELICON HALL, N. WOODLAND AVENUE, 1906. Once a private school for the pampered, this experiment in co-operative living established by Upton Sinclair generated much unwanted publicity in the day's yellow journalism. The 62 resident middle-class intellectuals and professionals (writers, editors, and teachers) shared a common kitchen, dining hall, and children's area. Sinclair Lewis was a college dropout hired as one of the household helpers that were to free the women from drudgery. The house burned in a fire of unknown origin just five and a half months later.

Brown Brothers

Helicon Hall in 1906-07 when it was occupied by Upton Sinclair, left, and Sinclair Lewis

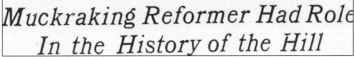

Muckraking Reformer Had Role In the History of the Hill

BERNARR MACFADDEN C. 1927. Macfadden was a physical culture fanatic advocating vegetarianism, periodic fasting, and strenuous exercise; he published ten newspapers, 13 magazines, and established "healthatoriums" and spas. After judging a contest for the most perfect female figure, he married the winner, a champion swimmer. Macfadden bought Campbell Dorrance's S. Woodland 1920 Italianate mansion and estate with ponds, tennis courts, and fountains, and added Englewood's first private swimming pool.

MANAHAN SANITARIUM AND RESIDENCE C. 1903. People came to Mable Manahan's on Liberty Road, near Greenleaf farm because this rural area was known for its healthful air. The inset shows Miller's Pond, once the site of the Westervelt sawmill, later a popular ice-skating spot. By 1907 the popular winter sport, coasting, was outlawed over Grand or Engle, or across the railroad tracks. Offenders were fined $5. Douglas Fairbanks, Mary Pickford, and Rudolph Valentino often used the Manahan property for filming.

ARMORY STREET. This brick row house is the scene for the 100th birthday party of Rev. Thomas J.B. Harris, pastor of Bethany Presbyterian Church from 1915 to 1927 and co-founder in 1918 of the League for Social Service Among Colored People, a precursor to the Urban League. He was the first African American army chaplain commissioned during WW I.

244 ENGLEWOOD AVENUE c. 1912. An artistic cement block house of rock-faced ashlar, this house was typical of the cement block houses in the Fourth Ward. The smooth corner quoining and the cement columns are unusual. In 1911, Smith and March's cement block factory, located at Englewood Avenue at the RR tracks, provided building materials for local houses.

PAPPIN HOUSE, C. 1867, HAMILTON AVENUE. Edwin Pappin, a local mason, built this small perfect vernacular example of 2nd Empire style. The one-and-one-half-story brick house with a straight-sided mansard slate roof, a center chimney, a three-bay porch facing south, and a one-bay porch facing east, is located near a church in a quiet residential Third Ward neighborhood. Local craftsmen often worked on East Hill mansions, then built scaled-down versions or copied details for their own homes. Some of the best examples line Cottage Place.

FAULKNER HOUSE. Faulkner was an active member and generous supporter of St. Cecilia's Church. Later the house became part of Temple Emanuel. The temple, which was founded in 1928, had been using various sites for services, including the Plaza Theater and the Busch Building on West Palisade Avenue, until the Tenafly Road property became its home. The temple's first pulpit was a 1929 gift of the First Presbyterian Church.

STAINED-GLASS WINDOWS. Englewood churches and Brookside Cemetery have beautiful stained-glass windows designed by the leading glassmakers of the time. Pictured are those at the First Presbyterian Church: on the left is the 1914 Resurrection Angel by the Louis Comfort Tiffany Studio using ground bits of ancient colored glass added to opalescent glass to achieve a unique luminosity; on the right is John the Baptist by the LaFarge Studio, in rippled opalescent glass. St. Paul's Church has windows done by the Tiffany, Lamb and LaFarge Studios.

TUDOR HALL, C. 1931. On the northeast corner of Engle Street and Booth Avenue, this Tudor-style apartment house featured a ballroom, restaurants, hairdressers, and laundry service. Tenants relaxed on roof decks surrounded by battlement parapets. Residents were thoroughly screened, even to their politics. The lovely interior garden, complete with fountain and formal gardens, "created an atmosphere of dignity and quietude."

DWIGHT MANOR, C. 1931, PALISADE AVENUE. This apartment house, advertised as a residence of "unquestioned elegance and sophistication situated on Englewood's prestigious East Hill," has become a distinctive neighborhood landmark. It was originally supposed to have an additional wing, making the building a U shape instead of an L, but the builder went bankrupt before completion.

MRS. SUSAN GRAHAM C. 1907. Mrs. Graham often drove to the strawberry fields in the western Englewood area. From 1850 to 1880, the Northern Valley was the largest producer of strawberries in the United States. Known for her beautiful, naturalized daffodil gardens, Mrs. Graham also taught sewing at the Social Service Federation. George Graham, her husband, was in charge of organizing the purchase of supplies for the British government during WW I.

MACKAY PARK, C. 1914. W.W. Phelps widened bridle paths through his woods for his daughter's enjoyment. These woods were also used for practice maneuvers during the Spanish-American War. After a portion of the woods became a park, George Graham and Police Commissioner Peter Duryea enjoy a horseback ride. They were both active in the Field Club, the Men's Club, and the Social Service Federation.

JANET GRAHAM C. 1916. Susan and George Graham's daughter is shown skiing on Lincoln Street, near her home. Miss Graham was quite athletic and won diving contests at the Field Club. Now in her nineties, she has remained active and currently volunteers at Lincoln School. She married David Van Alstyne, who was awarded the Croix de Guerre for valor in action during WW I. He later headed an investment company, was state senate Republican leader, and a founder of the Bergen County United Way. The Van Alstynes bought the Vermilye house on Chestnut Street.

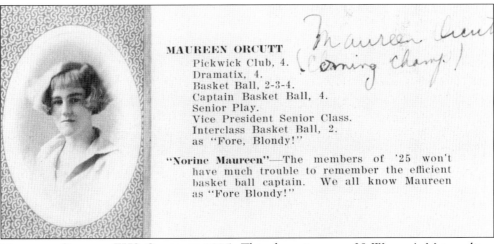

MAUREEN ORCUTT
Pickwick Club, 4.
Dramatix, 4.
Basket Ball, 2-3-4.
Captain Basket Ball, 4.
Senior Play.
Vice President Senior Class.
Interclass Basket Ball, 2.
as "Fore, Blondy!"

"Norine Maureen"—The members of '25 won't have much trouble to remember the efficient basket ball captain. We all know Maureen as "Fore Blondy!"

MAUREEN ORCUTT, EHS CLASS OF 1925. This champion won 28 Women's Metropolitan Golf Association titles, including the sister-brother tournament eight times with her twin brothers (Sinclair-5, Bill-3). She won the Canadian Women's Amateur Champion and USGA Senior Champion, was an LPGA Hall of Fame member, and was named to the New York Sports Hall of Fame. She wrote about golf and reported for *The New York Times* for 36 years.

WEDDING PORTRAIT. Hyman and Jennie Wides had one daughter and four sons, and each of their sons had a store in Englewood: Morris's fruit and vegetable store on Palisade Avenue catered to the wealthy; Dave's fruit and vegetable on Palisade Avenue was for the average customer; Isaac's liquor store was on Lafayette Street; and Sam's grocery later became a bar and grill. According to Jeanette Wides, Sam's daughter, "Everybody knew the Wides. When we went out, our parents knew who we were with before we came home."

WIDES CORNER. For the Italian, Jewish, and African-American families who lived here harmoniously after the turn of the century, Wides Corner was an important local shopping area. Sam Wides, in front of his grocery store at the corner of Lafayette Avenue, had the following opening day specials in July 1912: "can of milk 9¢ and strictly fresh eggs 25¢ a dozen—telephone 230." Later, the grocery made its own ice-cream sandwiches, though the flavors were limited.

NUTZHORN WEDDING. Adolph and Emma Nutzhorn had seven children. Bernard died in infancy, and Anna died at an early age after a failed romance. Ina, Emma, and Dorothy worked as legal secretaries, lived together, were active in the Lutheran church, and traveled extensively. In this wedding picture, Minna (nee Nutzhorn) and her husband, Hugh Dryburgh, are attended by her brother Carl Wilhelm and his wife, Lorena (nee Robbins).

STILLMAN AND HOAG GARAGE, 200 ENGLE STREET, 1908. Car buyers of this era took delivery of a box of parts, not a shiny new car. Partners Walter "Colonel" Stillman, a wholesale dry goods salesman, and Daniel Hoag, a wholesale grocery supplier, used this garage as a sideline, to assemble cars. In 1917, Stillman and Hoag became a franchised Buick dealership. Today, Stillman Automotive, expanded and relocated on Grand Avenue, is still run by the Stillman family.

SHERWOOD PLACE HOME C. 1878. In 1908 Nathaniel Norton, an insurance adjuster, paid $7,500 for this Queen Anne-style stone house with two fireplaces up and two down. Henry Brinckerhoff lived next door; the Westervelts lived around the corner; Clifford Beers, author of *The Mind that Heals Itself*, lived across the street. Four generations of this family have lived here: Norton, his daughter Caroline Norton Hazelton, her daughter Caro Hazelton Beaumont, and currently Caro's daughter, Natalie Beaumont.

BABY CARO C. 1909. Shown with her mother, Caroline Norton Hazelton, Caro grew up to attend Dwight School and Vassar, work at Babies Hospital, Columbia Presbyterian, and was the first president of the Englewood League of Women Voters. She married E. Butler Beaumont, who taught humanities, math, and science during his 45 years (1928–1973) at Englewood School for Boys.

HAZELTON FAMILY, C. 1911. Hugh and Caroline Norton Hazelton are seen here with daughters Caro and Sylvia. Caroline was a teacher. Hugh, who designed the electrical system for the Hudson Tubes, was president of the Englewood Board of Health in the 1920s. The Board of Health closed the schools during flu epidemics, closed Englewood to outside children during the 1920s polio scare, and held the first rabies inoculation clinic in conjunction with the Englewood Kennel Club, an offshoot of the Field Club.

WESTERVELT GIRLS, 1902. Marian was seven and Noeline nine in this picture. Their mother died three years later at age 38, leaving the girls with their stern father, banker Arthur Westervelt, and, according to Noeline, an unhappy childhood. Noeline's yearbook at Dwight School named her best looking in the class. Her "destiny" was to be a chorus girl but she became an interior designer. After her marriage, she became a well-known antiques dealer specializing in English silver and hunting prints. Marian, "quiet and pretty," worked as a secretary and lived on Hillside Avenue.

MICHAEL AND BESSIE LEBSON AND FAMILY C. 1914. The Lebsons lived behind their original Palisade Avenue jewelry store. Later they bought a home on Armory Street. When they moved to Elmore Avenue, Michael bicycled to work. Their five sons, shown from left to right, are: Isadore, dentist; Abram, lawyer; David, jewelry store owner; Samuel, insurance broker; and Jacob, jeweler. All worked and lived in the Englewood area for years.

EMANUEL AND MARTHA HECHT, 1908 ENGAGEMENT PICTURE. The couple had six sons and two daughters, and set up a store on Palisade Avenue in former Firehouse #1. Four of the sons worked in the store, first called the Paris Store and later E.W. Hecht Army and Navy. In 1916, ladies coats were on sale for $5.98; corsets, 98¢; boys' school pants, 59¢; and Fruit of the Loom Muslin, 10 3/4¢ per yard. An ad stated "Ladies Trimmed and Untrimmed Hats a Great Reduction, Call and Convince yourself." They also gave S&H Green Stamps!

FIREHOUSE #1. "It was a glad day (1899) for every fireman when, inspired by enlivening music, we marched out of our old firehouse into the new on Palisade Avenue." A hook just below the imposing bell tower gripped cotton jacketed hoses, letting them dry. By 1902, the firehouse owned four horses, the largest named Dan for, ambiguously, Mayor Currie or Councilman Platt. In 1901, citizens living in Nordhoff met to organize a firehouse in their neighborhood. The first night they enlisted 21 volunteers, who operated out of Peter Spindler's woodshed for the first months. Members organized Englewood's first Firemans' picnics and balls to raise funds to build Firehouse #3 (pictured right).

THE PALISADE AVENUE FIREHOUSE, 1923. The firehouse was almost fully motorized, with the exception of a Seagrave horse-drawn wagon. The city had a full-time paid department, had invested in three fast-moving expensive trucks, and no longer needed neighborhood associations. In 1926, the department moved again, around the corner to William Street. E.W. Hecht bought the Palisade Avenue property and opened the Paris Store.

HIGHWOOD. On the Northern border, originally called Highlands, Highwood voted to join Englewood when it became a city in 1899. It had a firehouse, shown on the right above (now an auto repair shop), a railroad station with a large freight house, and a school on Orchard Street (now apartments). In 1885 Highwood had trotting races at the Englewood Driving Association Grounds. Winners could take home $60. The barn (barely visible on the far right) is the same as below.

HIGHWOOD VOLUNTEERS, 1903. People in the Highwood section of town, fearing they lived too far from the existing firehouse, organized their own volunteer group. The city gave $4,500 to finance a building on East Ivy Lane. In the photograph, the men of Company #2 lined up behind their firehouse next to the Dutch slope-roofed barn. There was also an "unmanned" fire company (#4) with twenty volunteers at North Woodland near Palisade Avenue. E.P.Coe donated the land for a portable firehouse with a small tower with a bell. It held a hand-drawn jumper reel and 1,600 feet of hose.

108

AMERICAN LA FRANCE AUTOMOBILE FIRE ENGINE. The Fire Department bought its first one in June 1910 for $7,500. It was faster than horses but couldn't handle much weight; more than two men slowed it down. The rest of the firemen had to get to the fire by a horse-drawn "express wagon." The chains on the La France's rear tires helped create traction on Englewood's muddy roads as well as in snow.

FIREMEN'S TRACK TEAM, 1930. John Quinn, far left, won the quarter-mile run in the annual Edgewater track meet. His teammates, L. Donahue and Westervelt, excelled in the broad jump. Shot put winners were Donahue and Stempler. Firemen also sponsored amateur and Golden Gloves boxing events in the Englewood Arena or in Madonna Stadium on William Street. Some finals winners received 15-jewel wristwatches; runners-up received seven-jewel.

POLICE. Frank Titus became chief under a Democratic township government (1899–1914). In 1906, salaries were graded by length of service. In 1910, constables and roundsmen were permitted to carry firearms. In 1914, the Bureau of Police Commissioners was formed, and examinations were formalized. A 20-man auxiliary force was authorized. In 1915, there were five calls for police action each day, with mad dogs a special problem. In 1916, a club was formed to train police dogs for war.

ACCIDENT C. 1924. A delivery van descending Palisade Avenue created a domino effect. By 1920, Bergen County had more cars per capita than any place in the United States, so a traffic Bureau was created. In 1925, Chief Michael O'Neil supervised 20 men, two cars, four motorcycles, and a side car. One motorcycle was demolished when a perpetrator was chased into and around the Oval Bar. The bar was also demolished.

WW I Soldiers. Henry P. Douglas (left), for whom the Henry Douglas American Legion Post #58 was named, was killed in France at the Battle of Champaigne. Two years later, through the efforts of the New York African-American veterans in his regiment, his body was returned to Englewood. A parade honoring his heroism took place along Palisade Avenue. Stewart Harcourt Trott (right) served with the American Expeditionary Forces in France, 369th Infantry, in 1918. Trott, born in Bermuda in 1889, moved to Englewood with his wife, Celestine (nee White), where they raised four children. He was employed by Pfizer Pharmaceutical Company.

Morell Birthwistle. One of the first Englewood men drafted during WW I, he was given a hearty send-off and served from September 1917 to May 1919. He served overseas and returned a first lieutenant. Morell was a partner with Alex Livingston in a real estate and insurance business.

JOSEPH MOSCIARO. He immigrated to the United States from Cosenza, Italy, immediately enlisted in the army only to return to Europe to fight for his new homeland in WW I. He became fluent in French, German, and English, adding to his native Italian. After the war, he patented a hot water heater. He was custodian at Roosevelt School his entire working career.

An obelisk and statue honoring WW I soldiers was erected in the Liberty Pole area and dedicated Armistice Day, 1924.

SEBASTIAN, LEO, AND MOO. Sebastian Lombardi and his wife, Saletta, moved to Englewood from Santa Caterina, Italy, in 1913. He is shown above, in 1926, along with his brother-in-law Leo, milking Moo, the family cow, at 545 Englewood Avenue. Along with Moo, two teams of horses for Sebastian's thriving stone-cutting and construction business, 200 chickens, and several lambs lived in the barn behind the house, keeping his family busy.

JOSEPH AND FILOMENA MOSCIARIO, LATE 1920S. Their friend Sebastian Lombardi built their Grant Street house for $2,700. He also built the neighborhood grocery store next door, owned by Filomena's brother Domenico Siciliano. The Mosciaros had twin daughters, Olga and Mary, who worked many years for the City of Englewood.

JUNIUS AND FRANCES TINSLEY. The couple and their children Madelyn, Junius Jr., and Curry are pictured in front of their Franklin. In 1926, the Tinsley family moved to 140 N. Dean Street, bordering the railroad tracks. Their youngest, Curry, who waved daily to the brakeman, was killed on the tracks at age six. Junius worked as custodian for Public Service until 1965. Junius Jr. retired as supervisor from the same company in 1988. Kenneth, one of the Tinsley's later three children, retired as Englewood Chief of Detectives in 1989.

MARY CLAY FOSTER, ENGLEWOOD, 1870. The name, place, and date are the only facts known about the subject of this elegant portrait. Other Englewood residents of the era, however, were well known. Unpictured in this book are: *ornithologist* F.M. Chapman; *Secretary of the Treasury* Charles Jordan; *photographer* Dorothea Lange; *artists* Chester Loomis and Brunelle Poole; *art historian* and *author* James Lord; *painter* Henry Ogden; *children's author* Anne Parrish; *violinist* Ruggerio Ricci; *winner of the 1908 New York to Paris Auto Race* Montague Roberts; *Secretary of State* George Schultz; *jazz musician* Leroy "Slim" Stewart; and *jurist* Harlan Fiske Stone.

SUFFRAGETTES? In the "Votes For Women" monster parade these men, dressed as women, entertained Field Club members as the holiday carnivals, fireworks, dramas, minstrels, vaudeville, games, and races brought families together on weekends. Evenings, bachelors and couples gathered around a piano, played the ukulele or mandolin, and danced.

FIELD CLUB POOLSIDE. For years, heated discussions about the "unsafe, unhealthful, and immoral" nature of a swimming pool tabled plans to build a pool, but in 1919, opposition softened and the pool became a popular place to encourage swimming skills and hold competitions. Inside the clubhouse, many girls attended Miss Florance's dancing class. Girls wore white gloves and ballet slippers; reluctant boys just wore the gloves to cover their dirty nails. Later on, they would come together again at the club's debutante parties.

RUGBY TEAM. This is probably the Field Club's first team, predating 1900. Right from the beginning, there were grounds for cricket, baseball, lawn and earth tennis, archery, and wheelmen. There was a brief attempt at a hare and hound chase, then nine-hole golf, bowling alleys, and a squash court. Club members competed avidly at regional and national events. Helen Homans won the National Womens Tennis Singles Championship in 1906, and Ethel Platt and Annie Coe won the National Womens Doubles Championship the same year.

MRS. DWIGHT MORROW (ELIZABETH CUTTER).
Educator, writer, humanitarian, and philanthropist
Betty Morrow was the first woman president of
Smith College since its founding in 1875. An 1896
Smith graduate, she helped raise its endowment from
$2 million to $6 million. She was the first woman to
be a trustee and elder of the First Presbyterian
Church, the first chairman and founder of the
Community Chest, headed Englewood's City
Planning Commission, was a life member of the
Woman's Club, and director of Elisabeth Morrow
School. In her spare time, she wrote lyric poetry and
magazine articles.

DWIGHT MORROW. One of J.P. Morgan's
Wall Street partners, Morrow served under
Presidents Wilson, Harding, and Coolidge.
During WW I, he was a skillful manager and
afterwards was put in charge of disarmament,
rearmament, and reparation arrangements.
After his Ambassadorship to Mexico, he was
elected by a landslide to the U.S. Senate. He was
being groomed to be the Republican candidate for
President when he died suddenly in 1931 at age 58.

Mr. and Mrs. Dwight Whitney Morrow

request the pleasure of your company

at their house warming

Monday, the thirty-first of December

from four until seven o'clock

Lydecker Street

Englewood, New Jersey

DWIGHT MORROW ESTATE. Mr. and Mrs. Morrow came to Englewood in 1903 living on Spring Street and on Palisade Avenue before moving to this Georgian Revival mansion, built (1926–1929) for them on 52 acres on Next Day Hill. Daughter Anne and Charles Lindbergh were married in this house; later another daughter, Elisabeth, took it over for Elisabeth Morrow School.

CHARLES AND ANNE MORROW LINDBERGH. When Dwight Morrow invited Charles Lindbergh to make a non-stop flight to Mexico City, he didn't realize he was going to be the matchmaker for his daughter, a licensed pilot and radio operator. The Lindberghs often flew together, pioneering new air routes to Latin America, Asia, and Europe. In 1930 the couple set a new transcontinental flight record. Born in Englewood, Anne graduated from Smith College in 1927, and wrote the popular *Gift from the Sea*, in addition to many other books.

117

UNITED GALILEE METHODIST CHURCH, 1916. After surviving slavery, the Civil War, and reconstruction, Revs. Frank McQueen and Edward Pearson moved here from Bennetsville, South Carolina, and began a "little Mission" Sunday School in the former's home. After the church formally organized in 1913, they mortgaged their houses as collateral to construct Galilee Church on Englewood Avenue. In 1958, the church burned and was rebuilt on Genessee Avenue.

REVEREND W.E. GRIFFIN. In 1911, Rev. Griffin became pastor of the newly organized Bethany Presbyterian Church. His first Sunday School Superintendent was Henry Wright, who helped to build the current structure and took care of it as its custodian. Wright's wife, Annie (nee Ackerman), was the founder of Bethany's Church Helpers. Under her guidance, the Cradle Roll began. Of the 22 children born to the Wrights, eight were baptized in Bethany Church, becoming life members. If they were too young to be in the sanctuary, these life members were cared for in the "cradle room."

ITALIAN MOTHERS' CLUB. The Workers of St. Anthony's Mission was formed in 1918 after a Lenten sewing meeting by the ladies of St. Cecilia's parish. The social activities of the mission included the Mothers' Club. It first taught catechism and sewing to children of immigrants. It assisted families who were ill or in need, and sewed first communion dresses and veils for the poor. Mrs. H. Hogg, who was president in 1924, would lend her car for church emergencies.

ST. CECILIA'S. Named for the fourth century patroness of church music, St. Cecilia's became a Carmelite Parish in 1869. A mostly Irish congregation financed a convent, a well-attended school, and, by 1912, the landmark white marble Romanesque church with gargoyles, built with the savings of maids, cooks, gardeners, and coachmen who worked "on The Hill." Shown above, a Memorial Tablet honoring the dead of WW I was dedicated, July 4, 1921.

119

SEWING CIRCLE OF THE SEAMAN'S CHURCH INSTITUTE, 1915. Finnish immigrants came to Bergen County in the early 20th century. Many men were carpenters or seamen; young women often became domestics. Before building a combination church and home, many of these women formed sewing circles and held services in an apartment on Thursdays, domestics' day off. The Presbyterian church let them worship, free of charge, on Sunday evenings.

FINNISH BETHEL CONGREGATIONAL CHURCH AND HOME FOR WOMEN, C. 1924. This church was founded by eight young women and their leader, Katri Tikkala, around 1918. In 1924, these women and other newcomers put together $500 and took out loans to incorporate a church. They built a church home on the corner of Hamilton and Waldo Place. It was later used for housing Finnish nursing students. This unique organization, founded and mostly maintained by women, was active until the late 1970s. It is now Refuge Temple Church of God in Christ.

REVEREND JAMES AND LELIA MCLEOD. Rev. McLeod was the first pastor of the Seventh Day Adventist Church located at Warren and Fourth Streets. Later, the church erected a spacious and modern facility on Englewood Avenue in Teaneck. Mrs. Lelia McLeod, an 1887 Tuskeege Institute graduate, was a licensed and practicing mortician in New York City. In 1921, she became a Red Cross worker in Englewood. The couple lived on Epps Avenue.

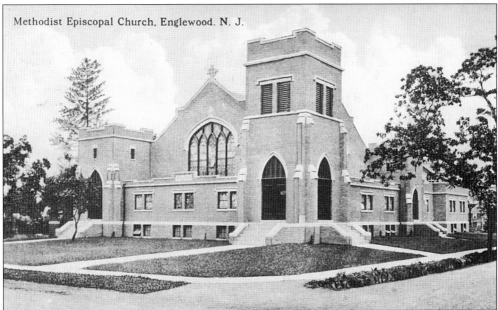

Methodist Episcopal Church, Englewood. N. J.

FIRST UNITED METHODIST CHURCH. The Red Cross occupied their early church on Grand Avenue during WW I, but immediately thereafter, congregants sold the building to the Cadillac Company of Englewood. Their new church, built on Tenafly Road and Demarest Avenue closer to their homes, embraced the modern concept of expanding a church into a community center. In addition to a chapel, it had space for a Sunday School, meeting rooms, basement bowling alleys, a gymnasium, and a kitchen.

AHAVATH TORAH. The first Jewish congregation in Bergen County began in 1895 with 25 Jewish families who lived in Englewood. A small building (18 by 30 feet) was built on Humphrey Street with contributions from Jews and Gentiles in the area. In 1912, a larger building (left) was built on Englewood Avenue. Later (right) it was renovated, removing the unusual domes. Ahavath Torah remained a synagogue until the Rock of Ages Deliverance Church purchased the building. Unfortunately, it was later destroyed by fire.

AHAVATH TORAH CHOIR, 1931. A group of young boys sang for the High Holy Days and Sabbath services. The boys, from left to right, included: (front row) Wallenberg, Cohen, Goldberg, Goldberg, Asch, Siegel, Schumer, Miller, Siegel, and Zeitlin; (back row) Zadonowitz, Levinsohn, Goodman, Cantor Gaslovsky, Silverman, Rosen, and Horowitz. A participant recalls, "It was hard to get us together for the picture, because we were all running around playing ball."

122

BETHANY PRESBYTERIAN CHURCH SENIOR CHOIR EARLY 1900S. Pictured are Temperance Kennedy, Bessie Bristow, Edward Ambleman, Priscola Boone, John Bristow, and Clemmens and Lucinda Smith. The Bethany Church is a member of the Presbytery of the Palisades in the Northeast Synod, and it is the oldest African-American congregation in Englewood.

ST. PAUL'S CHOIR C. 1930. Music has always received considerable attention and given great pleasure at St. Paul's Church. Dr. Howard Robbins, rector from 1905 to 1911 published several hymns. Rector Dr. Russell Lynes (1922–1932) wrote about church music. James Corneille trained a large boys' choir. John Harms, for whom the former Plaza Theater has been named, was a later choir director.

MEMORIAL HOUSE. Built in 1916, this red brick Italianate style building donated by William M. Imbrie housed clubs for boys and girls and a nursery school. In 1922, Memorial House joined with the Civic Association to form the Social Service Federation. Hot lunches were provided to schoolchildren for 15¢. During the Depression, the price was reduced to 5¢.

MEMORIAL HOUSE GUESTS. As the Depression continued, funding for the nursery school became depleted, and the trustees were going to close the school. It was saved by Miss Elisabeth Morrow, who volunteered to assume all responsibility for costs. Pictured here, in front of Memorial House, are (left to right) Trustee Mrs. Henry Esther, Secretary Miss Anne Smith, Amelia Earhart Putnam, and Elisabeth Morrow's sister, Anne Morrow Lindbergh.

PARADE C. 1916. The parade included prize-winner "Companions of the Forest," Sons of Italy, Women's Christian Temperance Union, Englewood Bird Club, Foresters of America, Community Club, and Knights of Columbus. Englewood has had many organizations and clubs, including the Shakespeare Club, Garden Club, Civic League, Rotary, Urban League, Odd Fellows, Bowling Club, Community Chest, Historical Society, and Friends of Englewood Library.

DOWNIE BROTHERS CIRCUS PARADE, 1931. The parade went down Palisade Avenue to Mackay Park, with a brass band and performers riding on top of the trucks. The first car of the parade is in front of Noonan's Meat Market, near the present location of McDonalds. Note city hall's pillars at the upper right corner of this picture.

BLOOMER'S BEACH IN THE PALISADES INTERSTATE PARK C. 1930. These bathers are among the last who will use this swimming area free of charge. Beginning in 1933, the park charged 10¢ admission to those over 12. During the Depression, this beach saw tens of thousands of visitors annually, most coming via the Dyckman Street Ferry.

UNDERCLIFF BEACH C. 1931. This beach, part of the Palisade Interstate Park (incorporated in 1900), was popular with both boaters and bathers. Approximately 2 million visitors came to the park in 1932. Nearby Ross Dock had 3,000 campers roughing it with hot and cold showers, sanitary sewerage, and a camp store. By 1943, both Bloomer's and Undercliff beaches had closed.

GEORGE WASHINGTON BRIDGE. In 1868, a group including J. Wyman Jones, Cornelius Lydecker, Nathan Johnson, and George Coe introduced a bill in the New Jersey Legislature for a bridge from Bergen County to Manhattan. Hudson County introduced a rival bridge, but Bergen won the charter. However, it wasn't until the 1920s that building the bridge became a reality, with this site chosen because it was the narrowest part of the river.

BUILDING THE GEORGE WASHINGTON BRIDGE. Under construction from 1927 until 1931 the bridge was built into solid rock 85 feet below the Hudson's surface. The bridge was, at that time, the longest and highest suspension bridge in the world. Fifteen city blocks long, its towers rise 604 feet above the water, supporting the four huge cables which in turn suspend the bridge roadway 200 feet above the water.

FDR OPENING BRIDGE. At dedication day ceremonies in 1931, Franklin Delano Roosevelt, then governor of New York, called the George Washington Bridge, "a testimonial to the high caliber of its builders." The governor of New Jersey was Morgan Larson. Swiss bridge builder Othmar Ammann and architect Cass Gilbert oversaw construction of the $59 million bridge.

BRIDGE TRAFFIC. On opening day, October 25, 1931, a total of 55,523 vehicles crossed the bridge. The advent of the bridge brought a flurry of real estate development, smaller housing lots and apartments. Englewood as "a high caliber residential town with elegant residences and every surrounding denoting wealth and culture" was now available to everyone. Today, over 135,000 vehicles pass through the George Washington Bridge tollgates each day.